THE LOST DIARY OF COUNT VON COSEL

INTRODUCTION BY

DAVID L. SLOAN

PHANTOMPRESS
K E Y W E S T

A DIVISION OF HAUNTED KEY WEST

© 2012 Haunted Key West

ISBN: 978-0-9674498-9-0

Inquiries: david@phantompress.com

Photos Courtesy of The Monroe County Public Library: Stetson Kennedy Collection; Fantastic Adventures, September 1947

Table of Contents

Notice To Readers

The content that follows are the words of Count Carl von Cosel, presented as he first wrote them in 1941. Some of the terminology is archaic, but has been left in its original form to maintain the integrity of his manuscript. Minor edits have been applied to the punctuation of the original text to enhance readability.

Portions of this publication contain detailed accounts of human decomposition. It is not recommended for children or those who may find the subject matter disturbing.

INTRODUCTION

Human obsession with death and the afterlife dates back to the earliest days of our existence. Vikings believed a righteous death would reunite them with fallen comrades; Greek Mythology tells of an underworld ruled by Hades and Persephone, and the Egyptians built elaborate temples for the dead while fine-tuning the practice of mummification to preserve their loved ones for eternity.

While it is easy to dismiss these customs and practices today, a look at our modern culture reveals that not much has changed with time. Key West is no exception. Above ground burials, haunted dolls, a history of Santeria… Even the name "Key West" comes from the Spanish "Cayo Hueso" – The Island of Bones. It is a name, likely applied by early visitors who arrived to find human bones arranged in intricate patterns across the beaches - the key word being 'likely.' It's a nice way of saying 'nobody knows for sure,' and this happens quite a bit in a town known for her eccentric writers, storytellers, fishermen and watering holes.

Key West is as famous for her legends as she is for her sunsets. We are a community that thrives on stories that become more spectacular with each passing year, but we also have a great respect for our history and our pasts. It is easy, however, for these lines to become muddled. Perhaps this is why the story of Carl von Cosel and Elena Hoyos has gripped our attention and remained on our radar for more than seventy years.

Carl Von Cosel was a self-proclaimed count, doctor, scientist and more. Elena Hoyas was a young Cuban woman dying from tuberculosis. The two met in Key West around 1929, and the events that followed made history.

On October 5th, 1940, Carl von Cosel was taken from his beach side laboratory to explain to the courts why he possessed a body that had been deceased for the better part of a decade. News from Key West quickly spread across the globe, earning von Cosel both fans and foes. Some labeled him a grave robber or necrophiliac, others, a hopeless romantic demonstrating love in the purest sense of the word. Opposing sides still disagree.

With each passing year, elements of the story are lost, but what remains are the words of the main character in this sordid tale of love after death. In 1940, Carl Tanzler von Cosel put his pen to paper to record a diary of his version of events. They were first published in a now defunct pulp comic called *Fantastic Adventures*, then lost to time. In the 1980's they resurfaced as *A Halloween Love Story*. When it fell out of publication, his complete diary was pretty much lost to the world.

What follows is the complete text of von Cosel's diary as it first appeared in *Fantastic Adventures*; a vivid account of his true story as it unfolded in Key West; all of it in his own words.

While many ghost stories are intangible, *The Lost Diary of Count von Cosel* provides a certain element lacking from so many legends. Tangible aspects. To this day, people walk the same streets von Cosel walked, sleep in the places where Elena's body was kept, and relax on the beach where a dark romance unfolded. Though it is impossible to validate every statement in this memoir, there is no doubting the sincerity with which it was written.

Scientist? Doctor? Count? Lover? Loon?

That decision is yours, but it is best made after reading the gripping, sometimes touching, often disturbing first hand account of a love that crossed over to the afterlife.

David L. Sloan
Key West, Florida
October 1, 2012

PREFACE

When in November 1940, I was finally released from prison, I was a very bitter man. Charges had been brought against me that I was a violator of the grave, a ghoul, a fiend of society. There was an avalanche of misrepresentations, of sensational press stories, which accused me of being a sexual pervert, a necromancer, and a maniac, while being confined for court hearing. Worst of all they had removed Elena's body, that body which I had treated, first to preserve it in its unearthly beauty, and then to reunite with its soul which always was with me in the scientific efforts of over seven years. What made these misfortunes even heavier was the fact that, at the time of my release, I was sixty-four years old, and had lost my employment through Roosevelt's retrenchment, had lost my home on the beach of Florida, which had been destroyed by hoodlums before my captivity, and with the war restrictions, found myself almost without means of existence.

With my whole life thus deranged, I lived for a time as a recluse amongst the rubble of my laboratory, using the airplane, which I had built for Elena, as a shelter. But then a strange and unexpected turn of affairs brought me back to life. I discovered that there was human decency left in this world. From all parts of America and even from foreign countries hundreds of letters poured in and thousands of visitors came to see me, not from idle curiosity, but from humane sympathy. In their eyes I had not committed a crime. Gradually faith recovered and hope returned into my heart. I decided that it was my duty to answer comprehensively those thousands of questions I had been asked in connection with my life, and my love for Elena. I decided also that it was my duty to clear myself in the eyes of the public of the false accusations which had been raised. In short, I found it necessary to tell my story, to remove this spectre of ignorance.

So in the cabin of Elena's airship, where her coffin had rested for so long, I sat down and wrote this account. My position was cramped in the pilot seat and made all the more uncomfortable, because war regulations made it necessary to remove the wheels from the plane, so that my quarters were not only extremely narrow but slanting backward.

I am no professional writer; I am not a poet; but I have a little gift of painting, and so I have tried to express in pictures what I could not say in words. In this manner, happiness of a kind came back to me; my life again has a purpose; although it is sad that these pictures (seen by visitors at my place) cannot be reproduced in this magazine.

Admittedly my experiments in resurrecting Elena were partly successful. Too often my work was interrupted and disturbed by outside circumstances beyond my control. But I am not giving up. I feel that the invaluable experience already gained lends itself as a reassurance that new experiments could be crowned with success.

Elena's body, true enough, is now interred, but her dying wish that she and I should, live together has been granted to both of us. She is with me as I write this, she advises me; in fact, it is her hand which, I feel, is leading my pen.

11

So then, I wish to thank, through this account, all those thousands of kindhearted and big-hearted friends who have come to my support in my hour of need. It was their faith in me which has restored me to new life; it is to them I dedicate this book, and to my Elena, as she was the first who visited me while in jail.

Karl Tanzler von Cosel

Key West, Florida, In the winter of 1940-41

CHAPTER I

THE GHOST OF CASTLE COSEL

I was born in Dresden, Germany, in the town house of our family, called the "Castle," but there was another castle, the Villa Cosel, out in the country and it was there I grew up. This latter manor had the reputation to be a haunted house and the White Woman, whom my mother told me had appeared from time to time during the past two centuries, was supposed to be my ancestor, the Countess Cosel, who died in 1765. Hers is quite a romantic history; moreover, since her apparition to me was the beginning of my relationship to Elena, I will briefly narrate her story:

In the Rococo age, when August the Strong (who became King of Poland) ruled over Saxony, the young Countess Cosel was one of the most celebrated beauties in this notoriously licentious court. She actually was the King's bride, as recorded. Family documents seem to prove that she was engaged to marry the young king. At the very height of her beauty and at the point of becoming a queen she fell in disfavor through the machination of some Polish Countess for reason of jealousy. August the Strong exiled my ancestor from his court and made her a captive for life at the gloomy fortress of Stolpen because she refused to return the certificate. For almost half a century she lived there in solitude which toward the end of her life impaired her sanity. For decades, however, she was able to find a new interest in life through the pursuit of alchemy, the hobby of the learned and the noble in those times. As a young man I went to see the Fortress of Stolpen (once headquarters of Napoleon) where the living quarters and the laboratory equipment of my ancestor were well preserved. Being a chemist and physicist myself, I can

14

witness to the fact that she must have conducted her experiments with great intelligence even if her quest for the Stone of the Wise was vain. Family tradition has it that her knowledge in chemistry enabled her to ward off several attempts on her life through poisoning.

As a young boy, however, I had no interest in the family tree and the existence of a ghost in the manor was never mentioned to me, nor entertained. True enough; at the age of twelve I had a dream, or rather a vision of a very beautiful girl in a white dress, reclining on a rococo settee, which I painted on a piece of paper then. My boyish interests were, however, entirely concentrated on electricity, on chemical experiments and on flying machines, astronomy, in fact on all phenomena of the universe.

While still at high school, fascinated by the saga of the Flying Valkyries, I built myself a glider plane. I tested this contraption from a, hill in the park, but then the giggling of the maids embarrassed me so that I continued flying experiments only after midnight to the alarm of the superstitious dogs of the peasantry.

Likewise, by the time I went to college, I had established in the Green Room of the manor a fairly big laboratory for high-voltage electricity. The garden hall I had converted into a workshop wherein I built one boat and two hot-air balloons made from Japanese silk which it took my mother and a needlewoman months to sew together. I had no interests outside science, music and paintings; girls did not exist for me, except formally, even as I went to University at Leipzig and I did neither smoke nor drink. Time seemed too precious to me for such pursuits of a momentary happiness. Engrossed in science after science I took, at the age of twenty-four, final degrees as Master of Arts in medicine, in philosophy, mathematics, physics, chemistry, etc., having passed nine different examinations beside the S.M.

I was sitting in my chair in the Green Room; piled on the large round table were writing materials from the college, books and laboratory instruments. Over the table there was hung a heavy kerosene lamp with a green shade which cast a bright light. There were outlined the static machines and all the other equipment. Toward the back the room was divided by a large curtain which enclosed my photographic darkroom wherein I used to develop the X-ray pictures I made. All was bright behind that curtain which I wanted to be very dark. To complete the picture; all doors, of which the Green Room had several, were locked, except the door to the adjoining music hall, which was furnished splendidly with a. Lipp piano, an organ, chairs, chaise-lounge, settees, Florentine table, life-size Venus de Milo and an easel on which there stood a picture I once painted of Judith, the beautiful Jewess who slew Holofernes. Besides there were several large oil paintings of Italian masters in gold frames hanging on walls, also 10-feet high mirrors and armor.

The hour was late, about eleven I should say; I felt tired but my day's work was not yet finished. Suddenly, without looking up from my papers, I noticed a movement near my side. It was a pencil lying on the table; it moved slowly half across the table. As I looked at it straight it stopped moving but the moment I turned my eyes back to work, I noticed from the corner of my eyes how it started again. Scientific training had taught me the first law in the observance of phenomena; don't change any of the existing conditions. This, however, does not apply here. I merely paid little attention to it and kept bent on my work. Then it lifted itself off the table, performing a few somersaults in the air and flying down to the floor. Now a matchbox started walking about the table, lifting itself, gyrating in the air; suddenly it went sailing to the floor also. Then there followed my books, a fact which was all the more ironical to me because these scientific books contained the laws of nature in which I implicitly believed. Yet, these venerable books took to the air, lifted by some unknown force, and crashed to the floor. The instruments on the table followed, one by one, except the few which were screwed to the table. My amazement I cannot even try to describe. Finally the entire heavy, oaken table with the papers in my immediate reach still on it lifted itself off the floor and floated upward as if carried by water. I was forced to get off my chair and retreat a little for safety. The table weighed more than two hundred pounds and I was afraid to get crushed if it came down. Up and up the table sailed, almost touching the kerosene lamp at the ceiling, and then it came swaying down, slow at first, but then with a crash which made the floor reverberate. I had retreated to he neighborhood of the large curtain which screened my darkroom. I almost touched the curtain, when suddenly flames flared up and came running along the curtain surface, gaining in intensity. Still more curious than frightened I moved away and noticed how the flames crept to the ceiling and then went out. Yet, there was no smoke, but there was a smell of burn, and as my fingers probed the curtain surface they were darkened by ashes.

I still tried desperately to find some reasonable explanation—the nearest matchbox was at least six feet away and it was closed—when another uncanny phenomenon manifested itself. There was a noise like the report of a gun from the direction of my static electricity machine. Walking over, to see what had happened, I found that all of the four huge central glass disks had been broken right through the middle. The outside glass plates of the glass case still were intact and so were the condensers. The damage made me really angry, the expensive machine was now quite useless. After a few minutes of gazing at it I heard footsteps coming through the adjoining music hall. I fixed my eyes to the door, wondering whether it could possibly be my mother because she only had a key to my door, when suddenly the door opened into the darkened room and to my utter surprise I found that my easel had just been overturned and the picture I had painted of Judith was lying on the floor with the glass splintered. And also the picture itself torn across the face through the middle.

I was not frightened or anything like that, I still believed in some kind of a prank or maybe that there was a thief or prowler in the house. My next step was to test all doors and windows which I found securely locked, and to search every nook and corner for a possible intruder. From the top drawer of my desk I had taken a loaded revolver which I always kept there. While still searching the bedroom I heard a renewed noise in the Green Room, and in returning there my eyes met the strangest sight:

All the chairs in the room had a lively time moving and poltering about, agitated by an invisible agency. No harm was done and the sight-was even funny. I realized that in the face of the supernatural I was rather a ridiculous figure, standing there, revolver in hand. So I put the revolver back into the drawer, sure by now that this was no man-made trick. But then the harmless dance of the furniture turned into something more malignant: I heard another crash, this time from inside the cabinet and as I opened its door, I found one of my mercury pumps, which I kept there, smashed, its fifty pounds of mercury running over the floor on which the splinters of glass floated. This was another heavy damage, running into hundreds of dollars, so my anger was aroused. "If this is, by any chance, the spirit of the Countess Anna who perpetrates all this, please give me a prompt answer."

I had hardly finished this sentence when my second mercury pump, fastened as it was to the wall, came crashing down to my feet, spilling also its contents all over the floor. "What is the idea of all this destruction? Why don't you tell me in a more civil way?" I exclaimed. After that everything was still. Nothing moved. It was as if the spirit or whatever it was, had understood. I looked at my watch; it was two minutes past midnight. Feeling that the demonstration was over and that there was nothing I could do for the present, I retired to bed, because everything was silent as the grave.

Upstairs in the dining room at breakfast next morning I told Mother about my nocturnal adventures, and it was then that she told, me the Green Room was supposed to be haunted for ages. Mother was as little

19

frightened of the ghost as I myself, but I found her very much interested. In fact, she asked me to install an electric bell which would connect her bedroom with my study, so I could call her immediately if the apparition should appear again. She declared she had heard some crashes last night and had felt the floor tremble at one time. The next night I invited several guests, all professors and doctors of Leipzig and Dresden, in the Green Room. One doctor came later bringing his wife, who was a good medium, but nothing happened except this lady, in virtually one minute was driven out by an invisible agency and had to be taken away at once. Otherwise nothing happened, so that the gentlemen departed. In the third night, however, I was mysteriously awakened at around 2 a.m. I hardly believed my eyes. There were, however, standing by my bed two women, one bending over my face, a tall lady with snow-white hair, a striking likeness to the portrait of the Countess Anna which I remembered so well. The second figure kept somewhat behind her, as if trying to hide, and the Countess held the reluctant younger lady by the hand. Bending still lower and staring at me, the Countess Anna addressed me as follows:

"I've been trying to attract your attention for quite some time, my boy. But you wouldn't take note. You were too much engrossed in your experiments. That's why I had to use some violence. Now take warning, do not entangle yourself with the woman represented on the Judith picture. Don't get ensnared by her. She isn't the one who is destined for you. Look here, Carl, I have brought you the bride whom some day you will meet."

I tried to answer something but I could not speak. I

20

had plenty of words, but I could not open my jaws. The Countess now stepped a little aside and at the same time she drew her companion nearer to me. For a very brief moment the veil parted from the shrouded figure's face. Spellbound I saw, framed in long, dark, black tresses, a young girl's face, so beautiful I can't attempt to describe it. For a fleeting second I saw the girl smile at me; a wonderful smile, but at that moment the Countess Anna detached herself from my arm which she had touched and the apparition quite suddenly disappeared.

Strange as this may seem, I was in no way over-excited. It all seemed very natural, if very wonderful, to me. With a feeling of relief and quiet happiness I just noted the time on my clock—two o'clock—and then fell back into sound sleep.

This then was the manner in which what most people would call the supernatural, entered into my life. I did not know at the time that this experience was to be formative for the whole rest of my life. My personal reaction to the experience was wholly scientific. Deny the apparition I could not. Rational explanation I had none. Determined to find a rational explanation, if I could, I started studying the metaphysical classics, in which, until then, I had not interested myself, and the more psychological and spiritist literature. This, however, I found to be of little help; it became increasingly clear that I had to navigate my own course into this vast, unexplored sea, though *Kiesewetter and DuPrel's Metaphysik* gave me a good foundation which is a necessity and safe guide in this field of ethereal phenomena.

One of my first steps was to visit again the Fortress of Stolpen where my ancestor had been confined. In the wing of the fortress chapel I found, under the rubble, a small square stone which may have been from the grave. Ivy had grown on the spot, a vine of which I had put into my pocket, as I dug into the stone rubble supposed to be her grave. On my return home I found this vine and planted it underneath the window of my study over the entrance of a subterranean tunnel. In my writing desk I also placed a piece of bone and a few splinters of wood which came from this grave of my ancestor. The vine grew fast and it gave me a strange feeling to picture it some day framing my window when I would look up from my work.

CHAPTER II

ULYSSES IN SEARCH OF ELENA

I, being a bachelor, set out on an Odyssey, supposed to end toward the Pacific, which in the course of many years led from continent to continent all over the world. I can refer to these years in only the sketchiest manner in this magazine account because all which matters is what leads up to my final meeting with the apparition of the castle.

As I went abroad a decade before the outbreak of the First World War, I was led by, some strange, irrepressible urge to the East. That there might be some higher purpose, some wise guiding hand in my travels, dawned upon me first on a certain date, when I went to visit the famous Campo Santo, that gorgeous paradise of a cemetery behind the city of Genoa.

There, all of a sudden, I found myself in front of an exquisite marble statue of an extremely beautiful girl, and was frozen in my steps because there was the most striking resemblance to the apparition of my promised bride. "Why, here she is in stone," I said to myself. "How very strange. Why could not God grant it to me that I should meet her in the flesh instead? Why is it that I must find her only as an effigy standing on a grave?"

I was moved deeply because of its minutely executed life-like resemblance. As I stood there I felt tears welling up in my eyes, a fact which embarrassed me because there were so many visitors around. But obviously all those sightseers were under the impression that I was a mourner, as indeed I was, and nobody paid any attention to me. Thus I stood in front of the statue for quite some time; all I could learn was that this beautiful girl had died at the age of 22, and that her name had been Elena. As if under a spell I

24

kept repeating that name, "Elena, Elena." And it was then that all of a sudden the figure of a live girl in the same white dress seemed to detach itself from the statue and slowly walk past where I stood, looking at me. There was no doubt in my mind that she was indeed the apparition of my youthful days and that she was alive. Automatically I took off my hat to greet her like an old acquaintance. Her eyes met mine, her lips parted in a gracious smile, and eager as I was to greet her, my lips spoke: "Good morning, my lady." Meanwhile the girl kept on walking slowly away from me and disappeared among the mourners in the maze of statuary. Only then did I regain power over my limbs and immediately

I started in pursuit, as I did not want to lose her. Racing up and down, through all the innumerable alleys of the vast cemetery, I searched for her everywhere, breaking through the throngs of visitors and stopping every one of the uniformed guards whom I met. "Haven't you seen a young lady in white? I've lost her; I've got to find her again." Darkness fell, the bells rang, the visitors departed, the gates of the cemetery were closed and I was still despairingly seeking for the girl of my dreams, mysteriously come to life and mysteriously disappeared again. The carabinieri of course believed my story; after all it happened often that visitors got lost in this jungle of statuary. They advised me to wait outside, while they themselves looked around everywhere. Finally I was told definitely that no young lady in white was to be found anywhere.

So that was how I found and lost my Elena the second time.

A little later, after Mass in St. Peter's, I went along the Via Appia and in the Catacombs of Rome I found myself by the grave of Saint Cecilia. She happens to be my mother's patron saint and Mother had told me that Saint Cecilia was my guardian angel who had dropped my cradle full of roses. So that was why I put a bunch of roses at her feet and I knelt to pray.

According to the Roman history of the early Christians in the time, of Nero: The dead were considered as still belonging to the society of the living, not as dead, only as asleep (like also in Germany in some parts); in Latin they were called *accersitus* which means called away.

After many travels in many a land I finally settled down after a fashion in Sydney, Australia, thirteen years before the outbreak of the First World War. There I was employed by the Australian Government as a civil electrical engineer and X-Ray expert. I had become a British citizen. I had a good salary and a pleasant home overlooking Darling Point. In the quiet harbor, right in front of my doorstep, there was anchored the big one hundred and ten foot, power boat, a former torpedo boat I had rebuilt for myself and which I intended to use for deep sea exploration and for fishing expeditions which often lead me far into the South Sea, archipelagoes. In these, my pleasant bachelor quarters, and in the night of the second of May 1910, I felt myself mysteriously awakened as if raised from the dead by a living hand. My first idea was that there must be a burglar in the house and for a moment I wondered why my dog did not bark, until now fully awake I remembered that my dog had been poisoned a few days ago. Now all the more suspicious, and connecting the death of the dog with some plan for burglary, being awake, listening, I heard distinctly footsteps coming to my house, halting at my door. Then heard a key being inserted in my door lock, the door opened and snapped back closed. Two nightlights were burning as usual in my bedroom and hall. Presently I saw a shadow moving slowly from behind the wall. It appeared to be a woman's figure, head and shoulders shrouded by a black headpiece like a lady looking halfway from the doorpost. Still thinking that the veil might be a burglar's trick, I sat up in bed under the mosquito netting. Then when the figure was retreating back behind the doorpost, both my night-lights were blown out as if by a shot. This could not have been through any movement of the air, neither caused by myself or anybody else, because my lights were in separate rooms, eternal room lights under glass and entirely windproof. In darkness now, I reached for my revolver on my right side, cocked it and listened sharp for any sound of approach while sitting very still until the rising light of morning showed sufficient outlines to see I was alone in my room, then I stepped out of bed. I went out to the terrace and around the house. I made a very thorough search but found everything in order, so that I decided that some kind of spook had entered my life again. This time I didn't like the prankish way in which it had extinguished my lights. In fact, the engineer in me protested against the unreasonableness of these manifestations. Cursing under my breath I went to my daily routine, as it was now daylight.

For more than twenty months nothing happened

except real burglary attempt, but in the evening of March 7, 1912, the real ghost returned, and this time to stay, when I was peacefully sitting at dinner in the early evening. For the last hour a storm was blowing outside, the galvanized roof of my house rattled with a deafening noise and through the windows in the fading light I watched the roaring breakers pounding against my bathhouse, and my boat riding at anchor, shuddering from the impact of the sea, lifting itself to every wave like a reeling horse. Otherwise in my house everything was as peaceful as could be, tea on the table and scrambled eggs, hot toast, cookies, bananas and meat, but no wine or whisky, a well-satisfied bachelor, all by himself. It was exactly seven p.m., when all of a sudden there was an end of the roar of storm and sea, glancing across the table I noticed a white-veiled form standing on the threshold of my door facing me, With my mouth still full of food I continued eating, too amazed to do anything else. At first I thought my eyes deceived me but the apparition stood there all right; after looking a second and third time there could be no doubt about its reality. It was a woman, about my own size, and I noted the rich, black hair unrolling over her shoulders, showing through the veils, so long it reached down to her knees. Even through the veil I could see dark eyes which fixedly stared at me; I also noticed that the light from out in the hall faintly showed through her form. A tremble of supreme joy and anxiety shook my frame. There she was at last, the apparition of Castle Cosel, my promised bride.

By the automatism of habit, I arose from my chair, addressed the lady with the conventional words "What can I do for you, my lady? What message may you have for me?

She did not answer but her beautiful face turned into smiles, the most heavenly I had ever seen. Still frozen to the threshold she stretched out both her hands to me, in friendly gesture like a child. As I walked across the room to meet those arms, I felt my hair raising and cold shivers running down my spine, the closer I approached her, and then I felt her arms closing around me and felt my arms embracing her. I cannot possibly describe the upsurge of a divine happiness such as I had never experienced before. There was a melting together in divine bliss. Her wonderful dark tresses, fragrant and caressing, covered us both. There were no longer any chills, only elation and warmth, filling my entire body. It was as if my feet went off the ground and she and I were floating in space. The intensity of this rapture was almost more than human nature could bear; yet I would have loved nothing better than to stay in this embrace forever; only at this very culmination of my happiness some substance evaporated.

The body of the girl dissolved in my arms. I still could feel her gown and still could smell the fragrance of "her hair playing around my head and body, but with the gradual disappearance of her form my arms fell limp and fear gripped my heart that perhaps I had lost her again, that perhaps she had sacrificed the very substance of her being, poured it all put into this one embrace.

Struck with the horror that perhaps it was I who had destroyed her in my arms, I stepped forward out of the room into the large hall and to my great relief I noticed that she had not disappeared, but her body reformed again. Only now she no longer stood in front of me but by my side, and as I moved she moved with me. Her feet, I noticed, did not touch the ground; neither did mine. With utmost caution I moved step by step and as I slowly walked around inside the house she went with me until we had returned to the door of the dining room, which also served me as organ room. Here her form detached itself from my body and now stood again on the threshold in the same attitude of a sentry as I had seen her the first time. For some unknown reason she did not enter this room. She smiled and seemed at peace. It was as if I addressed an angel who was forbidden to speak but understood all I spoke in any language in my strange attempts to evoke some kind of a response. Now this might sound silly, but it all served me as an exploration of her human abilities so I offered her to share my food, invited her to a seat at my table. I thought perhaps the offer of a cup of tea might tempt her, or that some small talk about my faraway relatives may bring an answer. I asked her permission to clear the table, and she seemed to understand. Having set my house in order, I found her still standing there. I made a gesture as if I were about to retire into my bedroom. She followed me to the bedroom and there she stood immobile on my threshold like a sentry or a guardian angel till dawn came. Then she followed me back to the hall where I went into my study and finally back to the organ room which she did not enter but stayed on the threshold. There followed the strangest week I've ever lived in life. I had the very strong impression that the ghost wanted me to go along with my regular work and ordinary pursuits. So that I went to work and when I returned, I found her waiting for me inside the entrance to the hall. She seemed to be glad to see me back because from the moment I entered the house she followed me around from the hall to the bathroom, from the dining room to the kitchen. Only when I went to sleep she stood near my bed all night. I could see her standing beside my eternal lamps exactly as when she first had come. Although she never spoke, she most always pleasantly smiled, and she seemed devoted to me, which made me indescribably happy. There was an incorporeal love between us which approached the divine. On the seventh day she left while I was in town and I felt her departure on my way home.

There was no explanation for her going, as little as there had been for her coming. All I knew was that she took my life with her, that wherever she went she and I would be united, and that she was indeed my promised bride. As she did not speak and tell me her name, I called her Ayesha, owing to her veiled garments of an Eastern Vesta Priestess and her spirit power.

I have no words to describe my sorrow over her loss; may it suffice to say that mental depression brought my health to a very low state, so that a fortnight thereafter I found myself in a hospital and remained there for more than three months, unconscious most of the time, under a combined attack of typhoid and malaria fever.

Finally convalescent, Dr. Breitner, the chief surgeon, handed me a bunch of letters which I had been unable to read in my illness. The first one I opened brought me the news that my father had fallen in a death coma on March 7, 1912, at 7 p.m., at the exact hour when the ghost had appeared in my house, and that my father awoke every day again at 7 p.m. until finally he had died on March 10th at 7 p.m., which was the exact, hour the ghost had left me.

In 1914 the First World War broke out and although I had become a British subject in the King's service, was in good standing with the community and employed by the government, the British saw fit to put me "for my own protection" into an internment camp.

I will not detail the next four years in the Trial Bay concentration camp, since this was covered by an article in the Rosicrucian Digest, beyond the mention of the fact that I spent a great deal of the time in constructing a pipe organ from sea-coast debris, with the help of some Buddhist priests also confined there. When the armistice was signed, the organ went with me in the ship, which sailed continually through storms. I feared for the organ, my most valued possession, but the ship did not sink, and in due course arrived at Dover from where we Germans were then trans-shipped to Rotterdam, two years after the armistice. I arrived still with my organ, at the old manor house in Saxony. During the fifteen years of my travels Father had died and one of my two sisters had married in America. Only Mother, now very old, and my youngest sister, welcomed me home.

When I was still in the concentration camp I had fancied, like most of the others that it would be possible to pick up the threads of the old life after the war. Reality, of course, was different, I was working on some new inventions, worked out while in the prison camp, but found they could not be used owing to war restrictions. Most of the old professors from my student days had died; the intellectual life at the universities which once I had cherished so much I found to be in a state of depression.

The whole country bore the stamp of defeat, I felt as if I were a burden to the meager resources of the family estates which were barely sufficient for Mother and sister. With my newly acquired patents of inventions, and *Reichs entechadigung* I decided to accept my mother's wish to go to America to my sister.

Because my sister lived with her husband near Tampa, Florida I chose the route by way of Havana, Cuba; on February 6, 1926 my ship, the Holland-American liner Edam, sailed from Rotterdam. The organ I built in Australia was to be a present for Mother, but then before I departed for America Mother herself insisted that I should take the organ with me in her memory. The voyage to Havana was uneventful; I kept pretty much to myself and felt more attracted toward the Spanish passengers we had because they were a more happy lot of people. On February 27th our ship entered the beautiful harbor, gliding past the old Morro Castle; I received my landing papers, went ashore and found by sheer good luck a very pleasant and inexpensive hotel room somewhere up town.

It was the time of the Carnival and all of Havana seemed to be intoxicated with the carnival spirit. I had never seen anything like it; originally my plans had been to take the ferry to Key West the very next morning. As it was I stayed four days, not to amuse myself but held to the spot by some strange, irrational hope that I could find my lost bride in this carnival crowd.

This was probably because there were so many beautiful ladies of the Spanish type who somehow resembled her, and because in this carnival time so many of them wore veils, and fairy-like dresses which made the similarity still more possible. As if I were a Spanish or a South American gentleman myself, I spent many hours on the Promenade where the band played against the thunder of the surf and against the mad rush of the big, open cars in which the Beauty Queens of Havana came sailing by, in endless procession. To stand there on the sidewalk was like sitting in a tremendous open-air opera house and to watch some wonderful circus perform. But, looking everywhere and always expectant of midnight when the veils of all these beautiful girls fell I never met with my loved one. The feeling persisted that she must be somewhere and I went back to my room when squads of little negroes started to sweep the streets from the refuse of the night's revelry, rolling -up giant six-foot balls of paper like snowballs in rainbow colors into the side alleys.

On March 1, 1926 I made up my mind that she was not amongst the ladies of the Carnival and that I would better seek my relatives in Florida. So I took the ferry to Key West. Disembarkation went without difficulty, but the telegram I had sent to my relatives had somehow failed to reach them. There was nobody to meet me and as the last train had already left I walked that night twelve miles under a beautiful moon along the railroad tracks; It was a strange sensation to be all alone in a new country where everything was strange to me and all the more mysterious, under the moon. Florida I thought was not as beautiful as Cuba; in the course of the next year I even tried several times to get away from there and back to Cuba. Each time, however, I felt myself drawn back to Florida by some mysterious force, the cause of which I was to learn in 1930.

CHAPTER III

THE BATTLE FOR LIFE

During my first years in Florida I had bought myself a piece of land, had fenced it in, and built a road across the land, and even laid the foundation for a house. The Florida boom, however, was quickly followed by a crash and it became necessary for me to earn a living by using my old faculties as a scientist. The Marine Hospital at Key West employed me as a pathologist and x-ray specialist; I built up a fairly well equipped x-ray department and peace of mind in scientific work until that fateful day of April 22, 1930.

In the middle of my routine work I received a call from the head office to go and take a blood test from a young senorita who as an outpatient had come for examination. I hardly looked at the patient as I entered the room. The first thing I noticed of her personality as I bent down to take a drop of blood from one of her finger tips, rather than one of her ears which were too exquisitely lovely to mar, was that her hand was unusually small; its long, tapering fingers, the loveliest I had ever seen. As the needle struck, the hand twitched a little and it was then that from my kneeling position I raised my head for the first time to say,

"I'm very sorry to have caused you pain; forgive me, please."

Her face had been hidden by her hand, so that I had hardly seen it as I first entered the room. But now she withdrew her hand to answer me and I looked into a face of unearthly beauty, the face of my dreams and visions— promised to me by my, ancestor forty years before.

I was so thunderstruck I hardly heard her saying:

"It didn't hurt much. Excuse my nervousness." Her voice was soft and sweet and child-like. It reminded me of a mocking bird's song in spring. She spoke with a Spanish' accent, yet her English was cultured and quite good.

Having performed the duty for which I had been called, I had no excuse to stay any longer in the room. Feeling very shaky, I arose and much too confused to say anything I merely bowed myself out, not knowing whether I was walking or dreaming. Back in my lab, I sat for quite a while lost in the memory of the apparition in the old castle, and in the Campo Santa, and above all my seven days with her in Sydney, Australia at the time of my father's death. Yes it was she whom at last I found in the flesh, and for proof that she really was alive I held in hand the little glass tube with a drop-of her red blood. A nurse brought me the record sheet for me to enter the results of my test. There was nothing much the matter with her blood but it gave me a shock to read on the top of the record sheet the "Mrs." before the name Elena Hoyos. So she belonged to somebody else. Was there a curse upon me that after this search of four decades had come to an end I should lose her again at the very moment I had finally discovered her, my promised bride?

Even so I felt indescribably happy. What, after all, did it matter if she belonged to another; hadn't I also belonged to another years ago? Our relationship had never been of an earthly nature. Over all these years what was there in a husband's name or even in a husband's existence? All this had very, little to do with me and Elena. The main thing was that I had found her and that she was ill and that I was best qualified and in a position to help her.

I saw her the very next day, when she came in for more tests and this time I took a radiograph of her lungs which brought me the painful revelation that she was suffering from tuberculosis. From the frailty of her figure, from the listlessness with which she sat, I had suspected that much the very first day. The certainty which now was gained increased my worries because our hospital was not adequately equipped for the treatment of lung t.b., yet some way had to be found to help her; a fierce determination to aid her, to bring her back to health was burning in my soul.

Both Elena and her mother could not fail to observe my deep interest in her case. They invited me to the family home and, needless to say, I went there that very evening.

It was a very small and rather dilapidated house to which I came; the family was poor. Elena's father worked in a tobacco factory. There were two sisters, all very different from Elena. Her mother, a good-hearted, if simple woman, and numbers of young people in all ages, whose relationship to the family I could never quite ascertain.

Elena, sitting very quietly, and obviously feeling far from well, in a chair in the kitchen, shone like the sun amongst all these lesser human stars. She and everybody else received me with great kindness and, best of all, the husband whom I had expected to find wasn't there. As the family secret was soon revealed to me, Elena and her husband had separated, as he had been responsible for her suffering. It was probably only human that this fact filled my heart with joy. Also it filled me with deep pity when tears welled up in the beautiful eyes of my Elena and she pointed to a car as it passed by the house.

"There he goes, he who was my husband. He now lives with another girl."

Impulsively I took her hand between mine and said,

"Don't worry over it, and don't worry about anything any more; from now on I am going to take care of you."

She thanked me with a happy little smile and like a child she said:

"Yes, doctor, I'm sure you will."

Days later I went again to her house, in order to take a blood test. This time I was led by her mother into her room. There, to my utter surprise and joy, I discovered hanging over her bed a picture of Saint Cecelia playing the organ, the same Saint Cecelia to whom I had brought roses in the Catacombs of Rome. Still treating me as if I were a teacher, which I indeed was, and she my little pupil, Elena said:

"That's Saint Cecelia, sir."

"Yes, and you know, Elena, she is my guardian angel, and this is the first time that I've seen her picture here in America."

"We too," said Elena, "are not Americans. We came from Cuba several years ago."

As in a blinding revelation I now had the explanation

for the spell under which I had watched the Carnival in Havana four years ago and I also had won the certainty that it was my guardian angel, Saint Cecelia, who had brought me and Elena together.

All this great inner happiness notwithstanding, my worries as a doctor mounted steadily. Since our hospital lacked the equipment I wished to use for Elena and moreover I considered the Florida climate as unfavorable for her condition, I proposed to send her at my own expense, of course, to some famous t.b. institution abroad where I was reasonably certain that she would be cured. This offer she refused because, in the first place, with the euphoria so typical with t.b. patients, she did not realize at all the seriousness of her condition. This left me only one choice; I had to procure at least the electrical equipment to treat her right on the spot. I wrote to several firms for the necessary apparatus and some of it I started building myself.

In the meantime I decided to give her radiation therapy with the hospital equipment, although the service outfit was not powerful enough for deep radiation therapy. Whatever was left of my spare time I spent on the completion of an airplane I had started to construct some time ago. Once Elena had regained her health this plane was to take the two of us to a South Sea island which I had discovered for myself during one of my fishing expeditions in Australia. This was a little paradise and my dream was that Elena and I should spend our honeymoon there. Every time she came to the hospital for treatment we took time out to inspect the plane together Those were moments of great delight for both of us, when we sat side by side in the little pilot's cabin and imagined how it would be when it carried us into the air and across the ocean.

"What name are you going to give to the ship?" she asked.

"I wish you would permit me to name our ship La Condesa de Cosel."

Elena blushed, for this was the first time I had intimated my wish to marry her.

"All right," she said, "let's name her 'Contesa Elena.'"

Her twenty-first birthday approached; I had high hopes now; that she would accept me as her suitor, as she had allowed me to buy the ring. I brought it over that day, hidden in a big bouquet of roses. I also brought cakes and wine and we had a wonderful day together, all the more so because nobody else seemed to have remembered the birthday of my Elena.

Next in importance to the ray-treatment was to build up her physical strength. Every day now I brought her fruit and some of the finest medicinal wine I could procure; I even went to the priest, because he was able to get the kind of wine for me which I wanted for my sick Elena.

With these combined means the tubercular infiltration for the time was checked, even with the minor equipment of the hospital, and Elena's general condition was improving. In fact, she told me that she didn't really believe that she was sick at all. I cautioned her as best as I could, but unfortunately her family, too, arrived at the wrong conclusion that their daughter was now cured and

41

that my continuation of the treatment was more or less a pretext to be as much as possible with Elena. To disprove this, one day I showed her my microscope and I showed her view slides with the little red rods of the bacilli. Naively, as a child, Elena fancied that I had painted those red rods on the glass. There was no use arguing because the poor child was enjoying a sensation of well-being, a result of the healing hormones which were stimulated by the x-ray treatment of the tissues. Not for anything in the world would I have robbed her of her high hopes, certain as I was that these were destined soon to fade again. Elena always undertook more work than she could afford in her condition.

Thus it was one day when the family invited me to the wedding of Elena's sister. When I got there late in the afternoon, the marriage ceremony was long since over, but an enormous party was in full swing. The little house was overcrowded with guests, all eating and drinking, and as the hostess for all these people there acted my Elena. She hardly took time out to take me by the hand to introduce me to the groom and guests, before she carried on carrying the trays around, serving the drinks, operating the gramophone, and doing a thousand other tasks. It was agonizing for me to sit there by the side of the bride, trying to entertain her as best as I could, while, through the clouds of smoke, through the laughter and the gramophone songs, I heard the dry cough of my Elena, who should rest her lungs above all.

The evening seemed like an eternity. It was near midnight when the guests departed and my exhausted girl sat down for a moment by my side.

"Elena," I said, "I admire you, you are the most wonderful hostess in the world. But this sort of thing just can't go on. Permit me to help you. Let's get married and let's get away from all this."

Before she could answer, her mother, whom I had not seen all evening, stood in front of us:

"No daughter of mine is going to marry an American. It is to be a Cuban, if ever she marries again."

With her head bowed, my Elena sat in silence. I took her hand and all I could say was:

"God bless you, and good night, my Elena."

The next time I went over, I brought her a pearl necklace. I had sent my big radio console to her house, hoping that good music would cheer her up. Whenever I found her in a depressed mood, which was often, I took out" of my pockets some new present for her; one day a large pendant of rock crystal, the next a pair of earrings and again a beautiful carved rose of pink coral on a gold chain, and almost every day I wrote her letters, wherein medical advice was strangely mixed with my love for her.

My darling Elena:

Please don't deceive yourself that, all is well, even if you feel that way, don't throw caution into the wind; your enemy is an invisible one, he can only be seen by trained, scientific eyes, and he can only be fought in a scientific manner. Please, darling, do not listen to irresponsible advice. I know there are quacks around who are suggesting all kinds of magic cures which have their common source in ignorance. Please, take the medicine I am

sending and do come back to the hospital for a new check-up. Dr.
Lombard, too, wants to see you. I am working on our airplane in
my spare time. It is now nearly completed and the next time you
come, I will give you the key for the cabin and we shall officially
christen it. And then too, I am already collecting all the things we
are going to need on our wedding trip. Silk dresses for you and a
bridal gown which is all white silk, and all the rest of your
trousseau, even lingerie and silver slippers and last but not least
all of your medicines, like chinosol and adrenalin, glucose, beef
extract and all the rest of it.

Forever yours,

Carl

It seemed, however, harder to get Elena to come over to the hospital. One day her excuse was that her father temporarily had no car. I sent a taxi over; still she refused, saying that she didn't trust the taxi company. My own car had just been stolen, so I borrowed another, but even when I came myself to fetch her, Elena would not come to the hospital. It dawned on me that some kind of an opposition had developed against me and the hospital people within her family.

That this was only too true was proved a little later, when again I found the house crowded with young Cubans, even, married with happy families, noisy with radio music and full of cigar smoke. I could not help to observe how Elena suffered and it made me mad. I told them they should at least refrain from smoking. This hurt the Spanish pride of her father. The old man made quite a scene about my interfering with his guests:

"My daughter is quite well and if you don't like the

smoking, why don't you get out of the house."

That settled things for this time at least. Elena's eyes followed me as I left the house as if to say:

"Suffer it for me."

Not to see her was torture and to be unable to do anything for her was worse. Night after night I dreamed of her, until after a week I got a little note from her:

Key West, September 10, 1930.

Dear Doctor:

I am so very sorry, because I know how unpleasant your last visit to our home must have been. Please, do forgive us, I'm sure father did not really mean what he said to you. He had been on edge all day and had been very cross with everyone. Please, understand that he didn't mean to be that rude. Both, my family and myself, would be only too glad to have you as our guest again. So, please, accept my apology for the other night, you must see us soon.

Your friend,

Elena Hoyos

After that, of course, I could not stay away. What did I care after all about what her people said or did? Her life was so much more important than a physician's pride.

Nobody smoked in the house this time. Nobody was there except Elena and her mother. I found my Elena in an appalling condition. She lay in a state of serious convulsions on her bed, trembling, and gasping for air. Her mother kept her covered with blankets. Determined to find out what had happened, I insisted on an explanation. The frightened mother finally came out with the truth: Elena had just been brought home from another doctor, who had been giving her injections for the past few weeks.

"What kind of injections?" I asked. "And who is the doctor?" She gave me an empty vial and named the doctor. This is a thing, of course, which many patients do: to go behind the back of one physician to another. This man was not a quack, but since he was not informed of my treatment and had started on a different one the two of us worked at cross-purposes and the harm to the patient was being done.

I got immediately in touch with the other doctor and we agreed that the injections should stop. The next test I was now able to make of Elena showed a decided positive albuminaria; her condition had rapidly worsened. It made me almost desperate, this ignorance and underhanded play which had undermined the resistance of my girl. Nor can I approve of medics who keep on pumping drugs into the circulatory system without constantly checking on the actual reactions. It means to work in the dark, besides it interferes with a healthy blood and has an upsetting effect to the curative effort. In this manner my poor Elena was needlessly made to suffer. Almost blindly obedient to her parents, like so many Spanish girls, she had followed their advice, trusting implicitly that it would be for the good. She was a good child, my Elena, too good indeed for these well meaning but ignorant people who simply had the old superstitious idea, 'the more medicine the better' and 'if one doctor doesn't help, another will'.

Worse even than this outside interference was something which I can hardly call by any other name than a conspiracy not to permit my girl the so much needed rest. Scores of cousins thronged the little house at all hours of the day and night; incessantly the radio blared and some sort of a celebration seemed always to be going on. Instead of, enjoying the quiet of a hospital which should have been hers, my Elena was damned to live as if in a railroad station.

For a long time now I had realized that there was only one way to have this radically changed, and that was for me to marry her. Time and again I told her so but she always gave me the same answer:

"But we can't marry, dear, I am not divorced yet, and even if I were divorced, you can't marry a sickly girl, such as me. First let me get well again."

"All right, my darling, I have patience if you have."

With much persuasion I managed to get her once more to the hospital. There I took another series of x-ray pictures which made it absolutely clear that her lungs had worsened. I also took a slow bucky-diaphragm picture of the trunk, including the larynx and thorax cavities. To make the best of it, I simultaneously gave her a good general radiation. Dr. Lombard, who knew of my great interest in Elena, came over and enjoined me in entreating her to come for treatment regularly—to no avail.

Knowing that we would reach this impasse I had already prepared to give her high frequency violet-ray treatment in her own house. Since I could not use hospital equipment for the purpose, I had built by my own hands a high voltage transformer for her and had bought another instrument from the Betz Company in Indiana for her use, but when on my next visit I proposed to have this apparatus, installed—at my expense, of course — the whole family turned against me. I was bluntly informed that my services were no longer required. I was accused of painting far too black a picture of Elena's health. It was hinted that she was making much better progress with the aid of patent medicines and that all this new-fangled electrical apparatus was devil's work.

That night I returned home a broken man. I had fought with all the persuasion in my power but the wall of faces, which confronted me, had been like, a wall of stones.

For the past nine months now I had overworked; my day belonged to the hospital, my evenings to Elena, my nights to work on the airship and on the million-volt transformer for Elena. This last blow, that I should be unable to attend to her, did the rest. I came down with Bright's disease and lay in the hospital for the next six weeks. Dr. Lombard's skill in the end restored my health.

All I could do, while I was helpless, was to dream of Elena and these dreams became more and more frightening.

Once I saw her, very pale and dressed in rags, walking alone behind a high iron fence as if of a penitentiary. I found myself on the other side and cried to her: "Oh, darling, I am so happy I found you at last. Run, darling, run quick, for farther down the iron rails I can see a little opening between the bars, it's just big enough for you to crawl through." She held her arms out as if to embrace me, I could drink one kiss from her lips. Then she

48

started running and came following me along; it seemed like an eternity until we arrived at the place where one of those bars was missing—and there she came out into my arms, kissing me.

When I wrote her about this dream, she instructed her sister to go to the hospital and tell me to dream no more. On Christmas night 1930 I dreamed I was in mother's home. Suddenly she rose, saying she would just go to the next room and be soon back again. She disappeared into the music hall, which was quite threateningly dark, and all of a sudden the roof collapsed and came thundering down and I saw mother buried under tons of stone and rafters. I rushed to her aid, searched everywhere to find a shovel and nowhere was there a shovel. From this dream I woke up, bathed in cold sweat and with the feeling that my mother was no more, which soon proved true enough when the death notification arrived. I must relate a third dream because of its connection with later events when I took my Elena out of the grave:

I had wandered into the countryside just outside Key West, and had come to a deep gulch with lots of underbrush on the embankment and water at the bottom. There I saw what looked like a bundle of clothing and discovered that it was a human body with the head buried in the mud. The dress looked familiar and as I quickly slid down the embankment, it really was Elena. I turned her over and her face was covered with blood and mud. I washed it with my handkerchief, always rinsing it in the water; At last her features became clear and I could see that only the bridge of her nose had been broken, but that there still was life in her. I took her into my arms and laid her on

49

the higher ground. There I did everything to bring her back to life and at the same time to clean her dress. I needed water, so I stepped down again into the gulch and saw all of a sudden, that there were more bodies lying in the muddy stream, men, women and children, but they were all dead and in a bad state of decay. I counted thirty-seven bodies in all. They made my hair stand on end because I thought they must all have been murdered and dumped and hidden here. So I fled and took the unconscious body of Elena in my arms to my laboratory. I had just placed her on the X-ray table to examine her for internal injuries when I woke up.

So began the year 1931 with threatening dreams and signs and portents. The invisible was warning me and in my convalescent state I felt forever more deeply depressed. This probably reflects in the notes which I sent Elena:

"Darling, if you have any willpower left, please, use it in the right direction, concentrate everything on your health. Please, do come over for treatment before it is too late.

"Let me see you again, Elena, I implore you. So often you have said that I am too old for you, but listen, darling, I never count my years, neither do I count yours. If you were a mummy, five thousand years old, I would marry you just the same. I swear; it's not for selfish reasons that I want this marriage but because I can do so much more than a boy your age. I can offer you my science, my experience, my capacity to save your life and this apart and on top of my undying love. You want to get well, don't you, and you want to see the world, don't you? You wouldn't imagine that this little Key West is the world, or that the life you are leading is anything like life could be. Oh, darling, I would take you to my South Sea Island or to the big cities of Europe or wherever you want to go. Only do come and let me care for you again.

"Darling, I've seen a girl dying in her home yesterday. Now I can't rest, I must tell you that she died from the same disease you have because she was already beyond help when she came from Habana Hospital, let not this happen to you, you have every right and every faculty to get well again. Let me implore you, take warning, please, do cooperate with us and do not waste away this precious time."

On February 2nd, 1931, to my indescribable joy Elena came to see me. She had put on her very best dress and she had cut off her beautiful long tresses and now wore her hair coiffured in the American style. Her presence did more for me just to have her sitting by my side in the waiting room than months of treatment. We couldn't say much, for as usual, there were a host of female guardians around. But then it wasn't necessary to say much, for our eyes did speak.

After she had left, the mailman brought me a black-rimmed letter from home. It went to say that my mother had died in the Lenten days. Now I knew what higher power had sent Elena to me on this day; it was to comfort me and strengthen me for this impending loss.

My health had returned but the depression of my mind remained because on my very first walk to Elena's house I found it deserted. Neighbors informed me that the family had moved but nobody would volunteer any information where to. From house to house I went and everyone shrugged shoulders so I couldn't help but realize that the neighbors had been warned not to reveal the new address to me.

I buried myself in work as best I could, automaton-like. Night after night I wandered through the town, peering secretly through the curtains of those innumerable little homes of the poorer sections, always hoping to find her and in vain. Her silence was wearing me down.

One, night an elderly, Spanish lady beckoned to me from the porch of her house and coming near, I recognized in her a woman I had seen with Elena's family.

"Your girl is very, very sick," she told me in a whisper. "The family has moved there-and-there. Elena is now in bed all the time, she needs you, but her parents won't let you come. I tell you what, doctor: it's a crime. Don't you pay any attention to the old folks. You just walk in and if you are still able to, help her. Wait, I'll just lock my door and then I show you the house where she lives."

I thanked her from the heart and then without a moment's hesitation I burst into the house which the kind lady pointed out to me. If anybody had tried to stop me, I think, I would have used violence. Right in the hallway I saw her sweet little face, looking straight into my eyes from a chair far in the kitchen corner. I cried:

"Elena, let me come in."

"Yes, doctor, do come, I'm so glad you are here."

She was dressed in a silk kimono I had sent her for Christmas, but I saw immediately the pale color on her cheeks, the light in her eyes and the emaciation of her body. The only thing to make me happy, of her appearance was the fact that she wore my diamond engagement ring.

Presently, of course, mother and some more of the family came into the room and stood there in silence. I simply said:

"Good evening, good evening, mother; I am so happy I found my Elena again. Tell me, what doctor is attending to her now?"

Angrily her mother burst out:

"I am her doctor now."

I laughed a little bitterly:

"You are some doctor, mother. I am sure you are a good nurse but not a doctor. I have come to stay. From now on you might as well consider me in charge for good."

I left them standing open-mouthed and turned to my bride:

"Please, darling, tell me whatever you wish or need at the moment and I will go and bring it to, you."

I should have said it before how very modest Elena was at all times. Though she needed practically everything, she would never confess to it, and so it was now:

"I don't need anything."

Taking her pulse I felt that it was weak, the breathing shallow, the general appearance was anemic and

a certain debility indicated disturbed blood circulation. .
Knowing how easily she took offense I did not tell her that,
apart from improper treatment, she had an abscess on her
leg caused by so many injections by another doctor. Lest she
should become over-excited I spent only a few minutes in
the house. Then, with a mixture of relief and sorrow, I left
and. spent the night with preparations for a determined
campaign to save her life despite all obstacles.

Before I could start new tests were needed. So the
next day I brought armfuls of fruit and little delicacies
which, as I knew, would stimulate my girl's appetite. I was
quite shocked to find how weak she had become. She only
took a little fruit for, when her mother brought her' a cup
of good chicken broth, I noticed how Elena secretly
emptied it out into the bucket near the bed. I also brought
her a jeweler's catalogue and told her to select anything she
liked in it, and which she wanted. This, too, was done to
revive her interest in life. She marked a bracelet watch, a
necklace and a wedding ring and told me:

"But only one, I do not want all three of them."
Naturally I ordered all the three for her. This gesture
brought the family into a more cooperative mood, so that
they were more agreeable when I brought my electrical
apparatus over for the treatment. Because I knew by now
the superstitions of these people and anticipated their
resistance when I arrived with the heavy artillery of the
million-volt transformer, I started with a small apparatus
and tried to get them used to it in a playful manner.

I placed the little inductor box and showed Elena
how it worked. It had a dry-cell battery for power and a

small movable shocking coil with silk cords and brass handles. Elena sat in her bed, her eyes bright with curiosity. I placed the handles and told her how to slide the coil for "weak" and then pull it for "strong" and how to operate the little switch. Then she took the handles.

"Do you feel anything?"

"No," she said, but my darling was cautious; she wanted me to test the electricity myself. After this was done to her satisfaction, I moved the coil slowly to strong until the current tickled her and she cried for me to stop. Delighted and thinking that it was great fun, she said:

"Call mama and Nana, Carl."

They all came and Elena played the joke on them and made Nana jump and so she made her mother. Gradually then the family, if it did not acquire much scientific knowledge of electricity, was at least convinced that it was fun and did no harm.

That evening I noticed for the first time that Elena coughed quite severely, was short of breath and had a sinking temperature. Throat medication therefore became my next step. I had prepared two kinds of throat sprays and solutions for rinsing. When I brought this, by good luck an old Spanish lady was with her. She was the only woman, who from the beginning had been on my side. Elena, I must say that much, was not an easy patient. Tiny particles of the spray in the form of mist settled on the sheets and pillows and Elena found that the odor did not appeal to her.

"Take the spray away," she said, "as far as possible. I

can still smell it." Then she turned to the old lady:

"Take this pillow out, granny, take the sheets out too and give me a new nightgown."

"Santa Maria," exclaimed granny. "What else?"

It was a pity she didn't like this fluid, it was most potent to counteract t.b. The other one had a more pleasant odor but then she disliked the taste. I had dissolved twenty dollars worth of pure gold and brought a sample of this solution for Elena to take a drop of it in her drinking water. She liked the looks of it, but again she couldn't stand the metallic taste.

My old sorrows of having my sick girl in what practically was a railroad station came back with a vengeance. Not with malicious intent but from sheer curiosity to witness all this strange apparatus I had brought and how it worked, relatives, friends, neighbors in droves gathered around the sickbed. They generally sat and lounged as near as possible on and around Elena's bed with the result that one night the whole bed broke down and my girl suffered bruises and a severe shock. She begged me to buy her a new bed, but-not another iron one. She wanted a wooden bed with high-closed ends for protection, so the people couldn't crowd her from all sides. Besides, her desire was for an inner-spring mattress and a dresser of her own, things she had never had before. For the first time we were alone that night; the collapse of the bed had put the camp followers to flight. The following afternoon the furniture company delivered the bed, the best and biggest bed I had been able to find. Soon afterwards there came another van with the largest mosquito top I had ordered and sheets and silk cushions in pink and blue and the dresser. Well, my darling was as happy as a princess in the fortress of her big, new bed and playing with a briefcase full of banknotes, which I had brought her checkbooks of the Reich Credit Bank and Key West State Bank, from the German inflation, with millions and billions of marks. I smiled, it did me good to see her happy as a child and enthralled with the illusion of being a multi-millionaire.

"Don't forget, that I still want to marry you, darling," I said.

"Oh, Carl, I wish we could, but I think I am going to die"

"No darling, you mustn't believe that, you won't be going to heaven for quite a while yet."

"I am not going to heaven, I am not good enough, I think I will be going to hell."

"In that case, dear, I will be going with you too. Wherever you go, there I'll go. But I am sure, that if you die, I'll take you in my arms and the good Lord will take us both into his heaven."

She motioned me to a little trunk which was standing in the corner:

"Bring this over, Carl, will you, please?"

Raising herself in the bed she took from the bottom of the little trunk a Spanish fan and opened it:

"I used this when I still was able to dance." At last she took out a couple of photographs. They were bridal pictures of herself and her former husband. She looked at them and then handed them to me with a gesture of despair:

"Take them away, Carl, it makes me sick to look at this. I do not know what folly made me marry that man. Cut him off my side."

She handed me a pair of scissors and I did her will, cutting the husband away from her side. She then told me to burn his picture in the kitchen stove. That was the first indication she gave that she did not love him any more and of her willingness to let me take his place. "

"If I must die," she said at last, "all I can leave you is my body. For I am only a sickly girl, so I can't marry you while I am sick. " But you will take care of my body after I am dead, won't you."

I promised I would and it was the most sacred promise which I ever made in life.

I kissed her then and laid her gently back into her cushions and put her feet high so as to get blood circulation back into her head for her breath was getting short.

This was what I consider as our marriage vow.

The latest test revealed that the laryngeal t.b. infiltration had made rapid progress. I found it necessary to move the ray-equipment I had bought for Elena into her room. My own home-built million-volt equipment I was unable to use because it weighed tons and would have necessitated the laying of concrete foundations in Elena's house. The machine I had bought was a high-power, high frequency medical unit with violet-ray equipment,

58

fulguration and throat examining attachments. It was strong enough to induce artificial fever.

This now I placed near her bed and plugged the connection into the light socket. I switched on the Tesla coil and hooked it up with one of the throat vacuum tubes. Elena watched tensely every one of my movements when I adjusted the apparatus, so that it showed only the faintest blue light in the tube without any sparkling. I then asked her to open her mouth wide and to hold still while I slowly inserted the tip of the glass tube until it almost reached her tonsils. For a while she was very patient but when she became nervous, she moved a little which, of course, had the effect of a little hot bite from the frequency sparks on her tonsils and tongue. I withdrew the tube whenever this happened and I heard her pathetic little complaint:

"The electricity has bitten me."

Towards the end of the treatment I noticed that her breathing had become normal and she had found great relief.'

I left the spark discharge on the wide gap for another hour. In this manner her room was charged with enough oxygen electrons for a whole night's sleep.

The next night I applied five-minute larynx radiation with the ultra-electrode tube to prevent dyspnea. Then exchanging the electrode for a surface tube I gave the outer surface of throat and chest an all-over high-frequency radiation for thirty minutes with medium strength. She enjoyed this as she would have a bath; it did her a lot of good because this radiation stimulates the tissues to new activity. Again there was pronounced absence of coughing

59

and her voice was stronger.

"I feel, so much better, Carl," she said, "perhaps I can soon go out a little and my first trip will be to church."

To keep her hope alive for this outing I went to Holzberg's store the next day and selected six Sunday's silk dresses for her and also silk stockings.

Tests showed a slight improvement. I began to become a little more hopeful. The next time I laid her on the autocondensation cushions and placed one sponge electrode on her chest, gradually increasing the high-frequency current until the milliampere meter showed four hundred. I let it stay there and told her to cry out when it began to burn. I watched her heartbeat and breathing and it was just ten minutes when she called:

"Oh, Carl, it burns."

Then I gently reduced the flow of electricity to zero. Her body temperature had increased between one and two degrees above normal. The pain in the chest had disappeared, breathing was normal but naturally pulse was fast. I covered her up with blankets, and told her to rest. Again she was all right for the night.

The next day her family told me with many complaints that Elena had nearly choked that morning in expelling a large plug from her lungs. Personally I was delighted because the good results I had expected from the diathermic treatment had begun to show. The removal of the plug gave her more room to breathe but it was too bad that the family interpreted this result just the other way around; ignorance, as usual.

"She don't need any electric treatment," cried her mother.

"You are running up a high electricity bill for us," shouted her father, "and who is going to pay for that?"

In vain I protested, of course, I would pay the bill for the electricity, whatever it was. The outcry was:

"Get all these devil machines out of our house."

I confess that I lost my temper:

"Will you take the responsibility to let your daughter die through your stupidity?"

Her mother burst into tears, covered her face and left the room. Worst of all, I heard Elena calling from the adjoining room:

"Oh, Carl, you have hurt mother."

"I am sorry, darling, but it was necessary to tell her the truth."

All this was terrible, because from now on I was again up against the stubborn family resistance which sabotaged my efforts.

For a few days the coughing was stayed but since Elena refused any further treatments, it now came back and so did the hoarseness which made her almost unable to speak. I had sent her a new radio with an amplifier microphone into which she could speak in a whisper and yet be heard. How pitiful it was that she would always gladly accept any such gadget but refuse what really could help her condition. Once she had made up her mind that she did not like a thing, it was final and I could only desist.

Pressure on my part led nowhere.

In her weakened condition her hearing had become very acute and hypersensitive. All the more did it pain me to see her suffer, when a radio across the street was always being played full blast and father filled the house with all the Toms and Dicks and Harrys of the neighborhood who were noisy and forever nosy about the equipment around Elena's bed, crowding her and cheating her out of her last chance in life.

I had to prepare for the emergency of an hemorrhage which now could be expected any day. I had tested my own blood and found that it matched Elena's. I kept my equipment for blood transfusion in readiness and sterilized at all times. I was ready to give half of my own blood as a last resort.

To relieve her at least from the radio blare, I had my little organ moved over to her house. Now I sat down evenings and played some of the soft, old harmonies such as Palestrina's.

Of food she took almost none except for fruit which she enjoyed, especially limes. She was able to eat those with relish, skins and all, and this gave me a little happiness because limes are a sort of antidote against the tuberculosis. Nature asserted itself in this instinctive craving for needed remedy.

If only her will to live could have been stronger. Do what I might, she was by now convinced and resolved that she was going to die and nothing I could say to the contrary would break this conviction. It was those many ignorant people who told her that tuberculous patients all die. Also she must have felt the serious deficiency of her chest inwardly.

One day, when I had lunch in a restaurant in town, I overheard a conversation in a nearby booth. People who couldn't see me talked about Elena's illness and that her family arid friends planned to have her removed to some mental asylum out of town because she wanted to become Catholic. I was horrified at that idea and so as to protect her against any trickery I immediately wrote the following statement:

To Whom It May Concern:

This is to testify that Elena Hoyos is my wife and that her mental status is normal. She is perfectly sane and under the medical care of Dr. Lombard and myself. I will not tolerate any interference or her removal to any institution or asylum.

Signed: Carl von Cosel,

Pathologist in the Public Health Service

I wrote this because my duty kept me at the hospital during the daytime. I brought her the letter that night and advised her to keep it always under her pillow and to produce it only if anybody should try to remove her from her home.

More than a hundred times throughout these trying months I felt sorely tempted to get some of the more obnoxious visitors by the scruff of their necks and throw them out of the house. Only the thought that violence of this kind was certain to harm Elena made me restrain. It

63

was particularly bad at mealtimes, when her father brought in some fat proprietor of a local bar who would keep on talking to Elena in rapid Spanish while she held her bowl of soup between her little hands and it was getting cold and her fingers cramped and she was too polite to eat. Only once after waiting twenty minutes did I muster the courage to say in plain English:

"Don't pay any attention to that fellow. Go right ahead, Elena, and eat your soup." She looked at me as if hypnotized and the fat man left in a rage. She ate the cold soup from the bowl.

The fascination of that barkeeper was that he flashed a loud diamond ring before Elena's eyes. In such matters she reacted like a child admiring it, so the only way for me was to outshine this diamond. I had one just as big on my own hand, but had never flashed it about. I put it on her hand next to her wedding ring:

"Would you like this one, darling?"

She nodded.

"Here you are, darling, I give it to you with my love."

She blushed with joy and would hardly permit me to take this ring to a jeweler just for a day to have it fitted to her finger.

"Look, mother, look here, now I have a real big diamond ring," she called happily, forgetting her misery for a time.

But when on October 11, 1931, I handed her the sparkling toy, she was so weak she could hardly smile and she was nervously asking:

"Did you bring my ring?"

"Yes, darling, here they both are."

I placed them on her finger, the solitaire diamond first and then the wedding ring next to it as security.

Calling her mother, and holding out her hand, she said:

"Look here. Mother. Oh, I'm so glad."

"You have five rings now," her mother said.

"She still has five other fingers left without a single diamond," I said.

Her mother laughed, going back to the kitchen.

Then I asked Elena if she had any pain and she said:

"No, I am all spent; father took me out for a walk to Celia's house (one-half mile) to see her radio, that's all."

"Darling, you simply must not take such walks; they drain your strength, you might collapse in the middle of the road. Get well and your airplane is waiting for you and we'll go together any place you like to see."

She promised it should not happen again.

Friday, October 16th, 1931, I came to the house and found that Elena was not there. Mother informed me that the father had taken her for an auto ride to town and she would be back in half an hour. In great anxiety I waited and when the old Model T Ford at last arrived her father carried my girl in his arms and put her in a chair. She had fainted on the way back and now she sat limp and pale, looking at me from sunken eyes as if to say:

"Help me, please, help me, Carl."

Life was fading fast.

Gently I picked her up and put her back to bed. There she took off all the rings from her fingers and piled them in a little heap:

"I won't have those now for very long."

I placed her in Trendelingburg position.

When the color returned into her face I left her to seek out the father. Knowing that this ride had very nearly cost Elena her life I was in a holy wrath which had to come out. I motioned the father, who contentedly was smoking his pipe, to corner with me behind the house out of earshot. There I told him without mincing words that another ride like this might spell the end of his daughter.

"But why do you think she should not take auto rides?"

"Because it will kill her, take my word for it."

He laughed aloud:

"Auto rides never will kill anyone."

Friday, October 23rd, I found my darling in a very exhausted state. She was too tired so I left soon and in utter depression. Yes, it is true that people can learn only by experience. But all too often they get the experience only after some irreparable harm has been done. In my distress my only comfort was that the family opposition against me now finally seemed to be broken down. I had hopes to

66

resume the radiation treatments. I had hopes that, despite the extensive damage, the lesions would begin to heal again. I had hopes that, when Elena was out of danger, we would get married. As long as she lived I never abandoned hope.

CHAPTER IV

ELENA'S DEATH

Sunday, October 25th, 1931, I had just finished my records after the day's work in the hospital and was just about to put on my black coat which I always wore for my Sunday's visit with my bright Elena; when the brakes of a car screeched in front of the lab door. Mario, husband of Elena's sister Nana, rushed in and told me breathlessly:

"Elena has just died, come with me."

Now I knew the cause of the oppression which had gripped me all day long.

We raced through the town. It was just five p.m. when, we reached her house. More than a block away we could already hear the people moan and scream. There was a big crowd around the house; we had to break a passage through the people.

Hoping against hope that something could be done I requested for all the people to get out of the room. Then I went down to my knees before the bed, I tested her breath and heartbeats. But there was nothing to be heard above the screams of the people.

I placed the faradic testing electrode on her neck so that it covered the nerve region. There was no reaction. That moment Dr. Galey arrived. He, too, examined her to find that all life was gone.

Mario tiptoed to my side and in my desperation I called out:

"If only you had come to me half an hour earlier, perhaps it wouldn't have been too late."

"I drove as fast as, I could," he mumbled. "What

69

more could I do?"

He had lost time trying all doctors in town but found none at home.

In halting words he told me what had happened.

On that fatal Sunday afternoon her father had taken her again on an auto ride to town despite my warning. She had dressed herself for the occasion in her new silk dress with all her jewelry and she had waved to all the friends she had met in the streets. Nobody had suspected that this was her last farewell.

Until finally she had collapsed in the car. Her father, supporting, her limp form, had driven home at breakneck speed instead of driving to the nearby hospital, where we doctors might have saved her life.

When he got home, his child was already dying. Her last words were for everybody to leave her room with the exception of a young woman who always had been her best friend.

Elena's jaws had dropped but her eyes were bright and clear. They had a faraway look and as I gazed into those beloved eyes, they seemed to become deeper and deeper like wells which, with magnetic power, drew me in. I could not tear my eyes away from her; I could look forever.

With shock I noticed that already she had been stripped of all the finery she had worn in death and that she was now clad in some cast-away and dirty old shirt which I never had seen before. Likewise I noted that all the jewelry which I had given her was gone.

My poor darling Elena; with her body still warm, she had been robbed of everything she ever possessed on earth.

Nana came in sobbing to ask whether Elena was still alive.

"No, she will never come back again," I answered.

Nana looked at her sister horrified:

"Please, close those eyes, doctor! Please, close them, I can't bear the look of them, I can't stand her stare, it drives me crazy."

"What a pity," I answered. "I could look into those beautiful eyes forever and ever."

But then I bent down and gently closed the eyes of my bride Elena, because I did not want anybody else to do this for her.

Nana quickly left to join the family in the next room while I sat quietly by Elena's side until the undertaker came.

Mr. Pritchard, the undertaker, at first discussed the matter with the father because there were documents to sign. I heard a great hubbub and confusion of voices and all of a sudden her father burst into the death room:

"I'm helpless, I don't know what to do, I'm in despair. Please help us, doctor. I know you thought the world of Elena. I know you will do this for her. See to it that she gets a decent funeral and a good place at the cemetery. I leave everything to you. I give you complete charge in everything to do just as you see fit. We poor people we have nothing. I leave her to you!"

"All right," I said, "but you should have left her to me while still alive."

He thanked me exuberantly. Then he called Mr. Pritchard into the death room and introduced me to the undertaker and told him that I was in charge of all the arrangements according to my wish and to that of the deceased.

I didn't think it was befitting to discuss these matters in the presence of my Elena. So I went with Mr. Pritchard to his funeral home. There I selected the coffin, the flowers and whatever else was needed. But when the matter of the dress came up I felt I had to speak to Nana, after removal of the body.

"Nana, why did you take away Elena's clothes? Why did you put that dirty rag on her? I want you to go and immediately bring her new silk dress, the last one I gave her. As to her jewels I will discuss that with you at a later time."

Of course, Nana started to cry but was sufficiently cowed so that after a few minutes she produced the dress. I handed it to Mr. Pritchard.

Throughout these technicalities I wondered over the fact that I was able calmly and deliberately to arrange all these things. The strange part of it was that with my brains I fully realized that Elena was dead but that my heart, with a far greater force, told me: "She is not dead." It was probably because I listened to the voice of my heart much more than to that of my brain, that the brain was enabled to keep on functioning in a reasonable manner.

The body had been removed from the house. In the funeral parlor I had placed a big heart of roses on the coffin of my Elena and I kept the vigil with her, then the coffin, with Elena and roses came back to her house.

At night I returned to the hospital for a few hours sleep.

October 26th, the funeral was set for 5 p.m. I worked all of the day. At four I closed my office and dressed. There was a surprisingly large number of mourners; masses of flowers formed almost a solid wall around my Elena's house.

There was nobody in Elena's room. I took my seat near to the coffin so I could drink in all her beauty for a last time. Beneath the closed lids her eyeballs seemed to have concentrated and they were looking straight into my eyes so I could feel their stare like a hypnotic touch. I sat lonely at Elena's side among the flowers during this last hour.

More and more people passed by the coffin depositing more flowers and the whole room now seemed to be filled with flowers and their overpowering fragrance. One thing which impressed me was the reverent silence of all these Latin peoples, who usually were so loud, being a Spanish custom. It was only I, however, who sensed Elena's spirit floating in the room, fairy-like or rather angel-like, from flower to flower. Maybe all those people reverently respected my silence communing with my bride in the casket, as there was no other living one inside Elena's death room.

I noticed especially one wrinkled little old man who deposited flowers, bent down and broke into tears at her side, and went out crying. Later I learned that this man had been Elena's former father-in-law. His was a human decency not for show, but for love of heart, which the husband lacked, for he never showed up.

The undertaker awoke me from my reveries; the funeral procession was about to begin, and everybody had to take seats in the cars waiting outside. I said to Nana: "She hasn't one single piece of her jewelry on her."

Thereupon Nana sobbingly produced at least the ivory necklace and the rose. I myself put on the necklace, and I wound the silver rosary around Elena's left wrist. Finally Nana also gave the black velvet felt with the brilliant clasp which Elena had loved so much and which belonged to her black silk dress, also one of the embroidered handkerchiefs which I had given Elena the day before her death.

At the very last moment, when the coffin was about to be closed, and everybody was out of the room, I took a letter from my breast pocket and put it under Elena's dress on her breast. Then I kissed her goodbye on the temple which was the one place which had remained uncontaminated by other kisses.

It was a very long procession, one hundred cars, which followed my bride and me to her resting place. All along the way there sounded in my ears Beethoven's Seventh Symphony. Mad as this must appear to most people, to me this funeral procession was like a wedding march, and the slow stepping of the pallbearers along the hearse in front of my car beating the proper measure for this symphony.

At church the organ sounded with, its angels' voices of a happy meeting in the better world. It was only then that I cried and cried from happiness. For now the long, sad, worldly struggle was all over. My bride was beyond malice, beyond unhappiness, beyond her pain. She was in the hands of God, the best, the gentlest hands that be.

Father Morreaux, who had but recently taken my Elena into the folds of the church, now spoke the last rites for her.

The coffin sank into its grave and when I thought, as did everybody else, it was all over, some Cuban, whom I had never seen before, indulged in a piece of fiery oratory wherein he demanded punishment for "the person responsible for her early death."

Whether he meant me I did not know and cared less, but I thanked him for his righteous thoughts and with a handclasp I assured him of my sincere support of his idea.

This then was what many, perhaps most people, would call' "the end."

A strange kind of new life now began for me. It was something like a rebirth after these last two oppressing and depressing years. Now at least nobody could take my Elena away from me. Although I could not see her any longer, I felt her presence all the time.

It was only natural that I went daily to the cemetery. What disturbed me there was the fact that, owing to the nature of the ground, hers was a shallow grave and by no means safe from water. In the dry season there was little danger, but I was worried at the thought of what would happen to my darling once the torrential rains started to come. There was no drainage of any kind in this cemetery.

It seemed unfair that her beautiful form should perish from the water; the only possible way to prevent this was to build a concrete vault around the coffin and to do it soon. In the meantime I kept the mound of the grave covered with a piece of tarpaulin which I took from my plane. The edges of the tarpaulin I secured to the ground with stones, and all the flowers I laid on top. Now she was reasonably safe, at least until I could build her a tomb.

Considering how often I have mentioned the strenuous relations between myself and Elena's family, readers will find it hard to understand why every night I went to her house.

It was the memory, of course, which drew me there, the atmosphere of Elena lingering on. But that was exactly why I felt great sadness in finding her room desolate with all of Elena's things removed from it.

When I inquired the parents told me that everything was burned, and that they abhorred this house where one of theirs had died and that they were moving to some other part of town.

I had the distinct feeling that I was not told the truth and that not all the things I had given Elena had been destroyed. It was not the material value of these things, it was the memory connected with them which made me say:

"Now, listen, if you are moving out I'm going to rent this house for myself, even if I have to buy it. Moreover you'd better be warned that the furniture and other things and jewelry I've given Elena were bought on the installment plan. If you want to keep these things for yourself I will notify the company according to the contract and you will have to pay the balance owing."

They did not like that particular idea and just as I had foreseen, the furniture was now produced from somewhere and placed back in Elena's room. Nothing had been burned except a few sheets and pillows and the trunk which had been the family's.

Delighted with the result I now told them:

"No matter whether you move or stay on, I'm going to live in my Elena's room, where she has lived and died because it is here that I distinctly feel at home in her presence."

To this they agreed and cooperated and from then on I slept in Elena's bed. It still preserved the sweet scent of her hair; for years I had not slept so well as I did in Elena's atmosphere. Nana had returned the old kimono last worn by Elena but she kept all the other dresses. I suppose she had need of them.

Regarding the jewels Mother told me that she had them all and none was missing and they were locked up.

"Keep them," I told her, "until the tomb is ready. Then I'll adorn her with all her jewels, because I don't want anybody else to wear them."

"Ah, but what's the use? There won't be anything left

of Elena but bones," she said.

"Don't you believe it, Mother. I'll take good care of her. I'll not permit her body to decay and if in the grave Elena should lose her hair I'll buy new hair and put it back on her head."

"Don't do that," said the mother, "don't use other people's hair; put her own hair back—I have some which she had cut off a year ago."

At these words she opened her dresser and took out, wrapped in paper, the beautiful long tresses of my Elena which had been cut off a year ago when she decided to wear her hair in the American style. This package she gave me, for which I thanked her with all my heart.

Having resigned herself to my determination, Mother was now a very much-changed woman indeed, and in a way so was the father too. He assured me that her room was now my own for the rest of my life. Both were satisfied that I would take care of Elena and were convinced of my undying love for her. I disconnected the radio in my room which I had purchased for Elena, that from now on was to be silent as a tribute to her death.

The father had become restless. He had no peace of mind and rarely was at home. Mother had become very quiet but the real reason for this was that she had fallen sick. There was something the matter with her circulation; she took treatment, by some Cuban doctor, but it didn't help. Instead it got worse. The heart became affected and the arms and legs were gradually, paralyzed.

I did not wish to interfere; after all she had every right to choose her doctor as she pleased. One night, however, her condition was so painful that she called me to her bed.

"Please help me, Carlos; the other doctor doesn't help me, but makes me worse and I am sure that you can do me good."

I made a careful analysis of her condition and after I had found the proper medication she was cured within a week. Now the last barrier was broken down; she was sincerely grateful for what I had done for her and even more for my care for Elena. At last there was someone who showed sincere attachment. She thanked me with all her heart.

All this time I used every free hour planning and constructing the tomb. I bought a larger plot around Elena's grave, sufficient for a family tomb. There I sat every afternoon after work on a little chair drawing plans and waiting for the mason who had promised to help me with the work. This man, however, with whom I had contracted, proved to be unreliable. He didn't show up, but kept me waiting and precious time was lost. Meantime the first heavy rains drenched the cemetery and I became very much concerned over my Elena, especially since I suspected odor developing from the shallow grave.

In desperation I went in search of another concrete worker; finally I discovered one and almost immediately we commenced work on the tomb.

But before we could start it was necessary to obtain a disinterment permit to remove the coffin from the site for temporary storage at a funeral home. It took us about a month to build the tomb, but then another month was needed to allow for the concrete to harden, and for the finishing of the interior another month.

Disinterment revealed that rains had indeed soaked the coffin and that moreover it had been partly crushed when a couple of gravediggers had trampled down the ground too hard after the funeral. It was with dire anticipation that I now approached the urgent task of taking Elena out of the damaged coffin and placing her into a new and stronger casket I had bought.

Toward this purpose the mortician and I arranged it so that there were no other dead in the morgue at the date for the re-bedding of her body. In preparation I had bought and brought all that could possibly be needed; new sheets, pillows, sterile cotton, gauze, chemicals and sprays. I also had built in my spare time an incubation tank and had placed it in the morgue just in case it should be needed.

This done I took a taxi and hastened to Elena's house to fetch her jewels which now were to be restored to her. Mother raised no difficulty over this; she gladly handed me the little box filled with the glittering toys and I hastened back.

After all the customary sanitary precautions had been taken, I opened the seals of the vault for which I held the key. The inner coffin, much damaged, became visible. Together we slid it out and set it on the concrete floor. The opening of the lid gave us considerable trouble owing to the demolished boards, lying inside on the body and because its lining inside had become attached to Elena's face and body.

Through careful work I was able to cut away this silken lining from the lid. The contents were now laid bare.

As the first step I sprayed diluted formalin all over the shrouded body in ample quantities. This was for disinfection and also to harden the body tissues before we undertook to detach from the skin the drapery which had become glued to it.

Decay had set in in a most disheartening manner. Only with the greatest care was I able to peel the pieces of textile from the body; this took hours. We then lifted the body out of the coffin and laid it on a table with a clean sheet. Having sprayed the body all over again, I now proceeded to sponge her, face with a specially prepared solution and also her hands and feet. With dismay I discovered that in view of the damage already done much more cleaning was required than could be done in the one night I had the morgue at my disposal.

Till dawn I worked with every energy, appalled at the negligence of the mortician who had failed to embalm the coffin itself which would have prevented much of the decay, because it was the coffin which smelled awful, not the body.

When morning came, my sweet bride was freed from all outward signs of decay and from that of odor. When the mortician came to work we placed her on thick layers of sterile cotton and after I sprayed her form all over with Eau de Cologne we now covered it all around with similar layers of sterile cotton. This done we lifted her into her new coffin and then this coffin into the new outer metal coffin which I had selected. This one was sealed all around with screws: The casket was of the airtight type, held together by a hundred screws.

The next day many people came to the funeral home wanting to see Elena but I had left instructions that under no circumstances were the coffins to be opened; this because I felt that Elena was not yet in a condition to be seen.

A few nights thereafter, when I could again have the use of the morgue, I took Elena out of the inner coffin and placed her into my specially made incubator tank. After this had been completely sealed, a task which took till midnight, I poured into the top valve of the tank a certain solution which I had prepared for her, both antiseptic and nourishing for body cells. This I kept pouring until the tank was completely filled. The tank was then placed into the casket. Now I felt easier; at least for the time being Elena was protected against further decay.

Now the tomb was finished and it looked more like a pleasant summer residence than a burial place and that it really was for my dear bride. This was exactly what I had desired for her and I felt sure that she would like this, her new little house. Onlookers passing by said they would like to move in it and make it their house.

The night before she was to move into her new residence I wrote a certain letter and in the morning took it with me to the tomb. The undertaker did the placement of the casket and then he left me, and I laid down the crucifix on top of it and lighted the little votive lights in the niche above her head, lights which from now on were to burn there day and night.

This done I closed the little curtains of blue silk which were to prevent curious people from peeping in, and saying goodbye to my bride for today I left her little house, carefully locking its door with three locks.

CHAPTER V

THE WOOING OF THE SOUL

Every evening at sunset I went to the little house I had built for her. I didn't to do this from a plan or with, any specific intention. I just felt drawn to the spot by some magnetic power which always increased toward evening and became quite irresistible when the sun set below the horizon. There were days when I had no intention whatsoever to go, when indeed I had pressing work on my hands. Each time, however, I simply had to drop everything to go to the little house in time for the rendezvous. With the moment I reached the cemetery I always experienced a sudden relief from the urge, the pressure which had driven me on. I had indeed a date, I felt it.

After a brief visit I usually sat inside the door completely relaxed and as contented as in the daytime I never was. Then I allowed my thoughts to wander, and they were all about my Elena. The troubled past reappeared before the mind's eye like a motion picture reel. At times I felt very tired in the consideration of this past and then it happened that I fell asleep.

Eighteen months after Elena's death had passed in this manner. There came a night when I sat inside the tomb, near the metal coffin on a little chair. It had been a sultry day and I had left the door wide open so that the refreshing coolness of the night could enter. The moist heat, however, was still in the little room and this was probably the reason why I fell fast asleep. Suddenly I was aroused by a loud, crashing report as if a cannon had been fired close to my ear. Thus roughly awakened I thought for a moment that perhaps some^ mischievous kid had fired a toy pistol to frighten me. But there was nobody around. Having patrolled the grounds outside, I returned into the tomb and now I noticed by the reflection of the streetlights outside that 50 locks which held the metal casket had sprung open. I examined them closely and it was perfectly clear that they had been sprung with great force arid all at once, and that this must have been the loud report which had aroused me.

Standing there in the semidarkness I smiled. For I remembered the prankish manner in which the ghost of my ancestor, the Countess Cosel, had manifested itself to me, smashing my laboratory equipment when I was a youngster. I also remembered how fond Elena always had been of the fun of a practical joke. This breaking of the locks looked, very much like Elena to me; perhaps she thought it funny to jolt her bridegroom in this manner who had dared to fall asleep in her presence.

Now I could clearly hear a tapping or a crackling sound inside, very distant, like nails of delicate fingers, probing and scratching a metal surface.

With spontaneous resolution I got the keys out of my pocket and quickly opened the remaining locks of the casket, and with some effort I succeeded in lifting the heavy lid. Starlight revealed that the inner coffin was still intact and sealed. But since I felt the necessity for closer examination and was unable to hold up the lid by my strength for any length of time, I looked around for some means to prop it up.

I happened to remember a piece of lumber lying around. I got it and now, lifting the cover once more, I could support it with the log with enough space in between to squeeze head and shoulders in.

I bent my ear to the inner coffin and listened intently. There was no sound, and I removed its lid altogether, putting it on the opposite side in the tomb. I tested every one of the hundred screws of the innermost casket; they were all intact. After screwing off the caps I tested the top valve of the incubator, which had a filter of sterile cotton. As I took this filter out, a strange and pleasant perfume emanated and spread all over the room. There was no pressure of gas inside. There was only this mysterious smell which resembled a hamine (fragrant chemical in human blood) and not any manufactured perfume. It was exactly like the healthy and agreeable odor of a young woman's skin, on a warm day. It simply was the typical odor which I loved so much of my bride Elena, and of her hair.

After a while I placed my ear against the open valve and after a minute or so I heard her voice. Very distinctly, in soft tones; it sounded so very much alive that instinctively I looked around everywhere to see whether by any chance she was standing somewhere nearby. She wasn't outside the coffin, of course, but unmistakably she spoke from the air inside, and she said these words:

"You do love me still, don't you? Tell me, am I really dead?"

"Elena, my darling, no you are not really dead. It's only your body that's asleep and your spirit is dreaming."

"Carlos, where am I?"

"You are in a little-house, darling, which I have built for you. I built it so you should not be disturbed, and be protected in your sleep."

"Is then this your house too?"

"No darling," I said. "I'm only here to visit you, and to wait for you to call me."

Minutes passed in which she seemed to think this over and then she spoke again:

"I wish you would take me with you to your home. I want to stay with you."

"With all my heart, darling. I will take you with me, if needs be, to the end of the world."

She gave no answer to this, at least not an audible answer, but it came to me as a divination that her lips kept moving down there and said something to me which I understood. That was why after a while I said aloud:

"Yes, darling, I will do exactly as you wish. When the moon changes it is to be. Then I will take you with me and you will stay with me forever."

There was no audible answer on her part to this. But a new wave of the familiar, the beloved fragrance of her sweet body arose strongly from the valve and filled the whole room.

A long time passed in which I had the top end of her coffin embraced in silent reverie. At last I felt that now she wished to go to sleep and it was time for me to leave her. It seemed cruel, however, to close the outer casket; so I left the lid standing open. With a last farewell "sleep sweet and

God bless you," I tiptoed out of the room.

Now this may sound surprising, but the fact is that coming home to my room I felt wondrously at ease, elated and at the same time very, very tired. I fell immediately, asleep, deeply and soundly as a little child.

From that day on I brought her flowers every night and other presents too. Well knowing how easy it was to make my Elena happy with some little thing, I always brought her a package of something bought on the way to her. One day it would be a few pretty handkerchiefs, the next a Spanish shawl, a comb, a vanity case. My greeting words were always:

"God bless you, darling, I am so happy I am back with you."

If this appears a strange or crazy thing to do, let me repeat, that once in India I had lain for dead myself and had thought I still were in my bed, whereas in reality, I had already been placed into the morgue. From this, my own case, and from many others on record, I knew that death is not the end of life and that resurrection from the grave is actually a possibility.

Naturally, the life of the dead is very different from normal. All the reactions are tremendously slowed down. There were days, when Elena's spirit remained perfectly silent and again days, when it would answer to my words after an interval of fifteen minutes or more.

A curious fact was that Elena's spirit showed all the curiosity of a very young girl, a curiosity which extended to the content of my pockets. Sometimes I carried things from the hardware store which I needed for my plane. Invariably then Elena would ask me:

"What is in that paper bag in your right coat pocket?"

And I would laughingly explain:

"Oh, darling; those are screws and little brass nails I need for your plane."

Often she was not satisfied with the explanation unless I spread the screws and the nails, or whatever it was, on top of the coffin for her to see.

By the same token she insisted on all the amenities of polite conversation. I never failed to greet her and to say goodbye in the ceremonious, Spanish manner.

Unfortunately my daily visits to the tomb and my prolonged stays there attracted considerable curiosity. Since the cemetery was located at the center of a public square with houses all around, it was easy for the innumerable children to lay siege on me. I realized that this was done, not so much from mischievousness as from ignorance and lack of consideration. But it was very annoying indeed. Finally I was forced to lock myself in the tomb and always draw the curtains, lest Elena's peace be disturbed. This reticence on my part seemed to provoke the kids still more. Their language became quite insulting, they kept their shouting up for hours, and when I finally left, there always was a crowd, staring at me from across the cemetery fence. Several times I had talked to the boys and asked them kindly to leave off, but it was all in vain. Not knowing what to do, and after they had gone so far as to throw stones against my sacred tomb, I complained to the police.

This helped for a while. I was sorry I had been forced to take this step, but to tell the truth it never had occurred to me that people could be so much lacking in reverence as to disturb the peace of the dead;

One Christmas afternoon I had come earlier than my usual hour in order to take a photograph of the tomb. Later, when it had become dark and I was sitting inside, all of a sudden I felt hands feeling all over my face and head. I could not see anything but the touch was the familiar one of Elena's. That night at home I developed the picture I had taken. I had taken thousands of pictures with this self-same camera and it had never failed. This picture however showed a white shape, resembling a human figure as if outlined in bright-white light, standing at the entrance of the tomb.

The constant nagging of the curious had irritated me so much that I changed my visiting hours farther into the night. It was the time of the full moon and the cemetery almost as brightly lit as in the daytime, so it could not have been that my eyes deceived me when on my next visit I saw a veiled, white figure at the entrance to the tomb.

As I came near, it started moving as if it had been waiting for me. I hastened to meet her but when I was only a few yards away, she disappeared through the locked door.

Inside the tomb I laid my hands on the casket and felt a strong electric current passing through my arm. The metal of this inner casket felt quite warm, almost of body temperature, whereas the outer casket was cold. The pleasing smell which emanated from the valve was particularly strong that night. As I always did, I held my hands over the valve into this beloved odor of my beautiful bride Elena. It was remarkable how long this odor clung to my hands; even washing would not remove it.

Within the next week the moon was waning fast, the nights became darker by end of the week, only a narrow sickle of the moon was left.

Ever since the moon began to wane, Elena had begun to sing in her casket with a very soft, clear voice which became just a little, stronger from night to night. It was always the same old Spanish song about a lover who opens the grave of his dead bride. I could distinctly hear and understand its every word.

This always lasted for no longer than perhaps ten minutes and then she fell to silence as if expecting me to speak.

"Darling," I would then say, "very soon now the moon will change, the hour approaches when I shall take you home with me. I will clean you and wash you and I will put on your bridal dress, with veil and crown and all. Thus, as my beloved bride, you will stay with me forever."

Two days before the moon changed, as I left the tomb and was already outside the cemetery, I suddenly had the queerest feeling that Elena wished to communicate with me. Without a moment's hesitation I turned around and felt my feet not like moving but like being moved back to the grave. Thus walking I remembered that there was a problem which for days I had pondered in my head and that probably it was this matter she wanted to discuss with me.

Putting my mouth to the valve I said:

"You know, sweetheart, your coming with me must remain a deep secret and I have been wondering how we can keep it a secret. You see, this cemetery is surrounded by streets and by houses. It has several gates, but they are all in full view of the houses and automobiles are passing back and forth past the cemetery at all hours. People are curious. They are quite used to seeing coffins go into the cemetery, but they have never seen the dead come out again. If they see us, people might raise hell. What are we going to do about this, darling?"

After a while, haltingly, but firmly, came her voice:

"Go out of the tomb, Carlos, and I will show you how this can be done."

Now standing in front of the tomb, I viewed with great misgivings the scenery around, the fact that the tomb itself lay in full view of at least a dozen inhabited houses, also in full view of the street. There was a fence around the cemetery but it consisted of single rails and iron spikes so that it didn't hide anything and the street was not farther than perhaps forty feet away. Between Elena's tomb and the street there lay only one more grave, that of a woman and it had a mound, not higher than perhaps two feet, so this too, did not offer any kind of cover.

While I was still pondering what possible solution there could be, Elena's voice spoke directly into my ear:

"You do it this way: when the moon changes, you bring along a very large blanket. You hang that blanket over the rail of the fence. Then nobody can see you from the street and from the houses, Carlos. The woman, my neighbor in the grave, she is my friend. She will be glad to help you."

Unmistakably Elena's spirit now used the full extent of its power over my nervous, system. She directed my every step; I merely acted like a radio receiver to the waves which came from her. My mind was utterly relaxed. All I could think was "Splendid, this is going to work." All I had now to do was to work out some means, to find some kind of mechanical device with which to move the heavy casket across the lawn to the point on the fence which Elena had indicated. I could not possibly carry it, because the heavy metal was altogether beyond one man's strength. Once I had reached the shadow of the blanket, the further journey would be comparatively an easy one. From this point on I could proceed along a lane between two rows of graves which offered protection from sight.

Automatically my feet had been moved under Elena's direction to the fence, where I was to hang the blanket. Automatically now my feet were being guided by her through the dark part of the cemetery. This rehearsal of the drama in which I had to be an actor the following night was so perfect that it seemed to me as if the coffin were already following me. I just listened to her voice which guided me, which directed me in every turn so cleverly that I was always kept out of sight from the houses and from the road. There was not the slightest difficulty; I proceeded as if I were running on rails.

Having crossed the cemetery in this manner, I felt my

step being halted at the far end. The dark shadow of a deserted house loomed up directly in front of me and within its expanse there was an even blacker shadow, square, an open window. There were houses to the right and left of the deserted one, but none of them had a window opening toward the cemetery. The cemetery fence ran perhaps three feet away from the wall of these houses.

Again I heard her voice:

"Into this window you shall lift me; Carlos, and I shall be safe in this deserted house and from it, later, you can take me away in an automobile."

"Yes, darling," I whispered. "Everything shall be done exactly as you say."

I felt that she had left me. Nearby I found a small gate, one which I had never seen before. Passing through it, I went home.

The next morning, I went at once to where that little house stood and found that it was real. I was fortunate enough to rent it for a workshop and storehouse. Of course, I occupied it at once to make sure of my possession. Now I felt a tremendous relief. Happy, I walked through town toward the laboratory. In a shop window, while walking past, my eye was caught by a small but strong cart with rubber-tired wheels like children used to play with. Here again her voice called:

"On this little wagon you will ride me along."

I went into the store, asked to be shown the wagon, and soon convinced myself that wheels, axles and frame were strong enough to carry the coffin. That certainly would help a lot in carrying the load. So I bought it and had it sent to my little house along with some other things such as carpenters' tools, etc. Evening came and as darkness fell, I went to the tomb, taking my dark blanket and black rain sheet with me. Then depositing it inside, seating myself beside the coffin I rested. Her spirit seemed now attached to my own, but remained silent, listening perhaps.

I spoke:

"Tell me, darling, will you truly come to me? Will you not fail to aid me at the last moment, as I must count on your support?" In a few minutes promptly came her reply:

"Yes, I will come with you and will help you."

At last now I was sure and contented," and I sang a little song for her quietly into her coffin. It was the old German melody:

"Come fly with me and be my wife, my heart thy resting place shall be," which I had written to her in a letter once before. And it was one of mother's favored songs.

I was prepared to risk my life, and to face any danger which would cross my path this night. There was no half way, this was clear to me. Once it was started it had to be carried out to a finish. This was my resolve. Besides, I did not know of a single person whom I could ask to help. Not a single human being I could trust who would be reliably discreet. And she would have to come out, if ever I was to take proper care of her.

CHAPTER VI

ELENA'S LIBERATION

At last the new moon had come. The night was pitch dark, and promises to the dead are sacred and must be kept. It was Saturday and most people were walking around town, busily engaged shopping and going to shows at 8 o'clock.

I waited till 8:30 and then went to my little workshop; opening the window wide into the cemetery, I suspended the little wagon out over the fence from the window, also two rubber cushions and a couple of short towing ropes. I then darkened the room, leaving open and locking the door behind me. I went out into the cemetery through that little street gate. I walked through the proper lanes between the graves until again I reached my window. I took the wagon down from the fence, along with the other things hanging there, put everything into the wagon and began pulling it along easily in the grass. But when it developed a very annoying way of rattling, I picked it up with its contents and carried it in my arms all the rest of the way to the tomb. The only illumination came from across the street. I unlocked the door of the tomb, and leaving the door wide open, I went down inside and spoke a few words into the coffin valve.

"Darling, I have come to fulfill my promise to you. Sleep now, darling, gently for a while, until you are with me. God bless you."

Then I screwed the valve shut tightly and took the inner metal coffin out gently, resting it obliquely on top of the larger outer coffin just for a few minutes. In the meantime, I took the dark blanket outside and hung it over the iron rail near the grave, exactly as she had advised. It was wise and excellent as I could now see, as it put the entire lower half of the entrance of the tomb into a protective black shadow.

On the threshold of the door I laid the rubber cushions so as to cover the uppermost step of the staircase inside. Everything was ready; before going down I took a last look around. I did not want witnesses. Satisfied that there was nobody prowling around I went down the stairs.

Inside, all of a sudden, the black crucifix above the head of her coffin shone into my eyes with a soft light which I had never seemed to have noticed before. I stepped toward it, made the sign of the cross, lifted it from the hook, kissed it: praying for my bride and for the protection of both of us, I promised to guard her and her sleeping soul and bring her back to safety with me.

Now I went to work, laying the crucifix on her coffin, and with new strength lifted it up high, I placed the foot end into the door entrance. The head end I was obliged to hold and push it slowly little by little further through the door opening until the entire length rested securely in the doorway. I now went up the stairs and pulled the coffin outside, behind the shielding blanket, into the soft grass. There, however, it could not stay for long, so I pulled it further around the corner of the tomb where it would be safer and out of sight. I slid the blanket from the railing and covered the bright, silvery coffin with it. Nobody could possibly see anything now because everything was black. I picked up the rubber cushions, closed and locked the tomb door.

My darling was now outside, ready and waiting the journey. Everything had gone well so far. With perfect ease I lifted the casket up on my little toy wagon, one foot high, with the rubber cushions one on each end, the blanket and crucifix covering the whole and partly trailing on the grass. With my ropes I tied the casket and wagon all around. With a short line attached to the beam I pulled the precious load from behind the tomb into the open section of the lawn in a straight line toward the dark portion of the main cemetery. Luckily, the wagon ran smooth and silent now under its load. It really was a wonderfully lovely journey through this black night along between the rows of graves, with my sweetest bride in her little metal chamber. Oh, it was immensely joyful and sweet, never to be forgotten. Serenely and calm I passed along, holding onto the reins of my hidden treasure passing noiselessly along by the two guardians of the Catholic ground. A wonderfully elated feeling took complete possession of my entire being, as though a second spirit had entered my soul. It seemed that a bodyguard of veiled angels had formed on both sides and were coming along with us and a great inspiration filled me then. It made me feel like a victor, holding the triumphal entry in a world forgotten and buried. I felt secure, protected and invulnerable. No matter what was coming against us now, nothing could harm either of us any more.

There was no place for the living here on this blackest of all nights.

All of the cemetery was alive with souls which came out of the graves from all sides, moving and thronging around us. It was indeed like a festival among the departed, as they moved up on all sides. It was like a great divine wedding march for me, taking place. It could not be a funeral march for all seemed happy and joyful and interested. In silent admiration watching as the white forms of angels filed past with Elena and me in their midst. They were everywhere, none blocking our way, but all of them melting out of our way. It seemed as if they had never had such a celebration in this cemetery before. It was as if all were delighted and desirous to help us. The little cart, for all of its weight, seemed almost to run by itself. It responded to the slightest touch of my hand, which gave me the impression of being aided on by friendly hands, reaching out of the ground.

At last we arrived and had to halt. The cart could go no further. Here on this spot the whole beautiful vision disappeared. The coffin had to be lifted off the wagon, I had to carry it in my arms to the fence and put it down in the grass on the other side. This brought me to within a few feet of my open window. The coffin was now under the window, resting in the grass; I also rested for a few minutes to gather strength for my last, great effort. Meanwhile I removed the cart and things to safety; nothing was to be left around to tell the tale. I drew my dark blanket across the windowsill with one end hanging out over the top of the wooden fence, to muffle any noise. Everything was ready now for the final lift, namely the raising of the head end, which was the heaviest, slowly up until it stood near the height of the window. This succeeded well; it stood Elena's body inside almost to an upright position, but this could not be avoided for just a few seconds. Then I lifted the coffin midway high above my shoulders and head, high enough so that it would clear the fence and blanket, and pushed it toward the open window. My back was toward the fence.

Suddenly the ground beneath my feet gave way. I lost my balance. It was as if all my strength had left me then. The whole load came down on my head, I crumbled under it and fell with the coffin lying on top of me, but my hands, still clamp-like, held onto my precious load. This meant a tragedy if my strength would not return to me. The falling casket had squashed my new black felt hat on my head, pinning me down. Quickly realizing the danger that threatened and breathing heavily, I summoned all of my remaining strength. It must have been more, it must have been supernatural strength which flowed through me—my own had all been exhausted. Again I tried, lifting the casket slowly high above my head. Rising up, and with my back pressed hard against the fence, I pushed the heavy end of the casket inside the window. There it now rested safely, while the foot end still pointed out into the cemetery.

For a while I rested, unable to move a limb, but thanking all of the good souls and angels from the bottom of my heart. I did not realize it yet, but my head and hair was dripping and saturated with sweat and blood. Also my hands, sleeves, shirt, coat and trousers were likewise wet and sticky. It soon began to smell, however, strong and obnoxious. This woke me up and warned me that there was something wrong. I soon discovered that the bottom valve of the coffin above me, underneath the foot end, had fallen out: I suppose, from contact with the top edge of the fence. I still felt something dripping on my hand and shirt, running down my neck and over the woolen blanket, hanging over the fence, against which I was leaning. As the powerful odor was quickly spreading, the dogs in the neighborhood began barking. I raised myself up to go inside the house and then pull in the casket. Locking the door and lifting the coffin and blanket carefully on the floor, I tilted it in such a way as to prevent any more liquid from flowing out, I then plugged the hole up tightly with cotton.

Now I closed the window and made a light. My blanket was such an awful smelly mess that I had to wrap it many times securely into a parcel. My clothing and I, myself, were in the same state. There was no way for me but to take all my things off and wash them and myself with alcohol, since there was no water in the house. Still smelling strong, but more like liquor now, I closed up the house and went home by a long round-about way, so as to give the wind and air a chance to take away the odor and to dry my clothes. The odor, however, did not leave me; no bath even would remove it from my body.

I left the coffin at rest in the little house over Sunday. On Monday evening I placed it on the cushions of a large sedan car and some airplane tanks, also propeller and parts for my airplane. Everything went fine; I arrived at the hospital grounds where the plane was without incident. This part of the hospital grounds, being behind the morgue, was quite deserted evenings. Undisturbed I had now moved my beloved into the cabin of the plane. She now had taken full possession of it.

CHAPTER VII

EXPERIMENTS IN RESURRECTION

Her wish had been fulfilled, and as Easter was close at hand, I made everything nice and cozy in her cabin. Her garments, bridal dress, veil, flowers, and jewels, shoes, stockings, everything was at hand, with plenty of money too. What more could my dearest girl wish for or have need of now? Gently, I slid the coffin aft from the pilot cabin into hers beneath the little curtained windows, which were all screened against insects. There was a tank of distilled water inside for washing and drinking, plenty of clean linen and sterile cotton. Everything medical had been provided for, including Carol Dakin instillation apparatus with solutions and chemicals. Her cabin was really the hospital of the ship. I started work, loosening all the hundred screws which were holding the cover of the casket tight. This kept me busy until midnight. The last four screws I left in place, one at each corner, because I intended to keep the casket closed until tomorrow.

The next night, snapping the latch of the door lock behind me, locking myself in, I pulled the curtains across the windows and knelt down on the floor beside the coffin. The last four screws were easily removed. I carefully loosened the cover and lifted it up and hooked it against the ship's wall. I can hardly describe the picture which unfolded before my eyes. It was a horrible and a saddening sight to look inside the coffin after eighteen months in the grave. It was disheartening.

"My poor darling, how you have been neglected. Of course you could not help yourself and no one came to your aid. May God forgive me if I could not come to your aid in time to save you earlier. In your plight your beautiful eyes broke and sank without anyone coming to bring you help. Your beautiful dress, it has decayed and now it mars your beauty."

My very soul was tortured when I saw her awful condition. I resolved that I would help her out of this awful mess at once. She was my beloved bride; my promise to take care of her was a sacred one.

With the greatest care, I now detached the uppermost layers, which were overgrown and eaten up with slimy moulds. I then got a large bucket and deposited rags into it until it was filled. Carefully peeling off all pieces around the head, face and chest first, I found that many pieces had become glued to the skin. All of those which did not come off easily, I left on her body to soak for the time being as it might injure her delicate skin, which I wanted to keep intact. The bucket was heaping full and heavy. It had to be removed quickly as the odor was overpowering. Then I prepared some soap solution and wetted all places and surfaces where rags were adhering to her body. Little by little the pieces loosened and came off, but not all of them that first night. Again and again I washed her body, tilting it carefully first on one side, then on the other, so as to wash the back and remove the rags from underneath. I also removed all uncleanliness from the floor of the casket. The bucket filled up once more and had to be taken out. When coming back, I rinsed her body and also the inside of the coffin thoroughly, but I used phenol solution this time for disinfecting and to remove the last traces of odor. After that, I dried her entire body, drained the coffin and sponged it clean and dry.

I placed new rubber cushions all along her body which was firmly held together and still showed evidence of living loveliness. For the first time now, I could find a little time to rest, to examine her body and study its condition more thoroughly. I looked into the deep fallen cavities of the eyes, like deep, empty black holes, I saw her dried up lips, slightly parted with her white teeth gleaming between them. And when looking so long and deep into those black openings, where once her beautiful eyes shone so bright, it was strange indeed; it seemed as if a pair of pupils were forming again, deep inside, and were looking at me as from the bottom of a well straight and seriously.

And then I heard her soft voice speak into my ear:

"Now you will love me no more, will you?"

These words cut into my heart, like an arrow, they set me on fire with sacred love for her. I assured her:

"Darling, I love you more than ever before. If it were not so, I would not have taken you to me."

Then, kissing her dry lips, and breathing deeply into her lungs until her bosom rose, I unpacked her bridal gown and covered her body with it. I draped her with the silk veil and adorned her head and hair with a golden crown. She looked so wonderful now, I could not resist. The wondrous spell and trembling with burning love, I sank gently into the coffin to her and kissed her as if she were alive.

Long I lay thus, holding her closely to me, the living and the dead united in love. The sweetness, of this was divine. Never had I dreamt that she had preserved so sweet and intense a love for me after being in the grave so long. Was it possible? I could hardly grasp or believe it, but here was the undeniable evidence. Life and death united together, eye to eye. Long and silent we lay. We needed no words. Words could not express the heavenly bliss that we were experiencing. We were two kindred spirits flowing together.

It was soul resting within soul. It was sweet and lovely beyond human words or understanding. God bless her soul and body.

Outside the night passed into dawn and still I held her head and body embraced. It was hard to tear myself from this wonderful heavenly spell. At last I raised myself and laid her gently on the cushions, promising to come back by night. Then covering her and lowering the lid carefully, without fastening it, I went home.

Throughout the day, however, I was haunted by conscience which said:

"Why didn't you stay with her? Why didn't you guard the ship?" It must have been her voice reproaching me. It was true, I had left her alone and unguarded, save by the cover and the ship. I could not visualize any danger to her though, as the cabin door was locked with triple locks. Besides I was badly in need of a cleansing bath before I went to work and furthermore, while cleaning the rags and mud away around her body, I had a number of microscopic slides taken with tiny specimen from various parts of her body, before cleaning it which I wanted to examine.

I went to the laboratory to examine them for bacteria. After I had finished the examination, I found her condition better than expected. There were no dangerous bacteria on any of the slides, just harmless infusoria and cilia. I felt sorry for any suspicion I may have had, although there was no real suspicion, only a little uncertainty. Anyway, I felt quite elated and happy over these results. Now I could sleep with greater peace and I think Elena also approved. My angel was pure, despite the mud and slimy rags in which she had been lying for so many months.

"Please, forgive" me, darling," I prayed. "You are an angel in death, you are purer than many a living."

I do believe in Brahman wisdom, which gives a recipe for any incurable disease: namely, die and be buried for one year, then you will be cured. But there are very few who want to try it, but whether they like it or not, they will all finally have to take it anyhow. But the destructive agencies used by the embalmer will preclude any possibility of coming back again. At last Elena had been cured of her disease. She died from pulmonary tuberculosis, and I had always found plenty of bacilli in my examinations. There was no trace of them now. For her to die was to be cured from t.b. She was relieved of that evil which had destroyed her earthly life.

It was the Easter morn of 1933.

It was her resurrection indeed when divine love has gently lifted my bride from the grave. How sweet she still was, even though some of the ravages of eighteen months in the grave had not yet been removed. I washed her frequently with perfumed soap and spirits of wine, and Eau de Cologne, still loosening many bits of clothing from her

109

body. Her beautiful hair also needed plenty of washing, as it was still partly glued together and to her scalp. By further examination I was not surprised to discover small maggots of the gnat larvae type which were feeding on blood around her head and ears and on the surface of the abdomen. I removed them easily with phenol solution. The surface of the stomach region and the lower abdomen was partly damaged and lacerated. I treated it with healing lotions and sterile packing, just like living tissue. I also bandaged up toes, feet, and fingers as they had badly suffered in the soil and threatened disintegration. I moistened these bandages with formalin to arrest further decay for the present. I did not find any bad discharges. There was no putrefication anywhere on the body, although parts of it showed indication of losing binding element of tissues. I also found deficiency of alkaline elements which had been used up by the cells. I applied a fine powder all over the moist surface of the body, supplementing the lost, calcium and sodium, neutralizing the skin to some extent, leaving it nice and dry and almost free from acid. Of course, I avoided any corrosives, alum, and other mordants on her. Instead I prepared solutions of a nourishing character with ingredients like olive oil or glycerine and others I wish to keep secret.

The idea of awakening her in this condition was out of the question. To my great joy, I noticed that her nose, which had been damaged through the handling of the coffin, had taken normal shape again after treatment and on exposing her to the air. When I first opened the coffin, the nose and eyes had apparently disappeared. Now the ridge was perfectly straight again where the bone had cut through the skin and septum. The outer nose had collapsed by the weight of the broken coffin lid when she was first buried.

Under the prevailing conditions, it was best to leave the body at rest. I must state right here, that I have seen living persons in worse condition than her body was now. If, however, she were to awake, it would cause another severe shock in her system, a second death probably, from which she could never awake again with this body. Only once is it given us; once only is it possible to live again in this body after death. When the body dies, the second time, nothing in the world is known, as yet, to bring life back again. The life in the enzymes has gone, and they are dead forever. The sinking of the soul into the body has the effect of preserving the vital power to resist the destruction of the enzymes. This action has proven itself sufficiently already. It also is apparent that there exists a connecting link between the metaphysical life forces and the atoms of the body, as the one influence responds to the other. It finally seems probable that the sleeping or dormant life force or soul is still being nourished or supplemented by the atoms and cells of the body.

For these reasons, and in consideration of her youth, I continued to give the body nourishment as long as possible. I also exercised a close chemical control over intake and exit to check on metabolism. There was, naturally, always a strong positive acid reaction from the tissues which often needed neutralizing. Youthful as she was, full of life, there was no fast dying of the forces of life, and with a little assistance, they will recover from the first shock, if the embalming process had not already caused their final or second death. It is too bad that the merciless, or rather murderous, ways of the so called embalming make it absolutely impossible for a poor soul, surprised by death, to return to an intact body. Some undoubtedly attempt to return, but only experience another, the second, death shock and are unable to start the demolished machinery again, so then they die forever.

Life is indeed a battle. This statement is in order, as really we fight from beginning to end, until, one by one, we drop out of combat. This may be only for a spell, unless some "well-meaning" creature cuts and demolishes our vital organs in the meantime before we have had a chance to recover. If only relatives and undertakers would act with more consideration for the dead. It is safe to estimate that many thousands of unfortunates have been killed in the past by post mortem embalming and too hasty burials. Modern science has advanced far enough to prove that death is not always final. In reality, death is just the first severe shock. Real or final death may follow, but not invariably. Of course, there are also many cases where recovery of life is impossible because the most vital organs are too far destroyed accidentally or by disease, and also some who even would not thank you for being brought back to life. In many cases, where death is not necessarily final, the relatives lose their heads. But the undertaker, who is bent on doing business, does not. Everybody is excited and rather impatient to get the poor unfortunate out of the way just as quickly as possible without further consideration. Of course, the undertaker is mainly interested in closing the deal, hence the indecent haste with which the body is removed and the embalming speeded up. This, although, I think, almost everybody would gladly pay the embalmer half the contracted fee, or even all of it, if their dear ones could be brought back to life. It would be desirable to give the dead a chance instead of depriving them of the last chance that God has given them. It is a fact, mostly forgotten in the hustle of this modern life, that thousands of certified dead have recovered from the grave. Thousands lying in graves would still be alive if humanity had more sense and tolerance.

As stated before, I had given Elena a letter when her coffin was closed by the undertaker. When cleaning the body after her disinterment, there was no trace of the letter to be found; it probably had been dissolved by the acids which were released by the body. Owing to the fact that no trace of it was found, I forgot all about it until later when looking through the records I found a copy of it, and as its contents have been transformed in actual accomplishment, there is no more reason for keeping it secret. It follows:

Key West, 26-10-31

(date of burial)

Elena, my Darling Elena:

My love for you is greater than ever. You are now free from all of your fetters, and you are free to go where you wish. Elena, please, come to me, sweetheart. I long so much for you, tell me, what shall I do? As I cannot live without you, will you have me darling? Then take me or you come to me and stay with me until I can go with you, my sweetheart, Elena.

I had begun feeding her body orally with nourishing fluids regularly every day. When I gave her too much of one kind, she usually expelled it, so I changed over to other types of food the next day. Finally the body adjusted itself to certain quantities which she would keep absorbed. Deliberately I used, only gravity feeding as the only safe way. By this method, the body recovered considerably and gained twenty pounds in weight. The treated tissues healed. After one month I removed the bandage and splints from the nose. It had knitted firmly and now she looked as beautiful as when she was alive. Lacerations on the cheeks and temple also had disappeared. I was obliged to correct her left arm which had been lying across the stomach when she was buried. The Negroes who had filled the grave had tramped stones and earth on the top of the coffin with such a force that they had broken the lid of the box and casket. This had settled down on this arm and on her face, causing a deep groove across the abdomen which also required treatment. The arm itself had suffered strangulation of its tissue vessels, as had the abdominal vessels. The whole arm had to be straightened slowly at the elbow and shoulder joint. This I accomplished by a counterweight with a cord over a pulley on the ceiling, fastened to a bandage on the wrist. It applied a gentle tension until the arm automatically took the required position below the hip joint. The groove across the stomach straightened itself but under treatment with hot solutions, in addition to warm internal infusions into the stomach and intestinal tract. It took quite some time, but I noticed with a great deal of satisfaction, how gratefully the body responded and returned to healthy form and appearance. Even the expression of her face changed to divine happiness. She did not require words to express herself. Her face was so much more eloquent than words could be.

Weeks and months passed. With the same routine of feeding and instilling vitamins into her body, she improved daily and even her living expression returned. It was my daily happiness and supreme joy to admire this phenomenon and I decided to make a plaster cast of her, so as to have a permanent and nonperishable record. In order to make certain and to be sure that one, at least, would turn out perfect, I made several casts. I discovered that the fine oiled silk which I had used to cover and protect her face, eyes, and hair, had fastened itself tightly to her skin. I left it so and painted over it with a thin solution of bees' wax and balsam. Being transparent, her eyebrows showed through delightfully. I did not dare to pull it off her beautiful face, as the plaster of paris, when setting, had pressed it so tightly against the surface of the skin. She looked as beautiful as ever and it looked like her own skin. It also proved an effective protection against ever-present insect pests and microbes. Later, after incubation of her body, I had to extend this same protection all over her body; only in this way was it possible to completely free her from those pests, which always doggedly found a way to attack her and cheat my rigid precautions, as I had to take her out of the incubator some day.

Her face expressed the divine peace she was enjoying, and happiness which I could only attribute to dormant life in her body which, like a crystalline solution will revert to its original form when letting it stand at rest. Her hair,

115

which had been flat and lifeless in her coffin, had become alive again, taking its own characteristic waves and curls. Her hair even regained its electric properties; being attracted to my hands when they came near it. No matter what the cause, it indicated life, though different than before. It does not react as quickly as ours because we're alive. The body reactions do not come as rapidly as before death, owing to deficient motor nerves. Still, the answer comes slowly of course because the body now stands under the law of eternity for which a year of our lives may be no more than a second.

CHAPTER VIII

THE LABORATORY ON THE BEACH

In the meantime great changes occurred in the hospital. The good, old commander of the Naval Station, of which the hospital was a part, had died. It had been he who had given me permission to build my airplane on the grounds. His successor, a much younger officer, promptly cancelled it. There was nothing for me to do but to move the ship to another location. I did not live at the Marine Hospital any more, though officially I was still listed as "on furlough." A place was offered to me right on South Beach where I could build my residence and airplane hangar. I had the plane trailed through town, with my Elena resting comfortably in her cabin. The way leads past the old home of her people, who once more waved a goodbye to us, not knowing of course how near their daughter was to them. It was a real triumphal ride for Elena as, in her flower-decorated cabin, she reclined behind the curtained windows, victor over her grave, radiantly beautiful and happy in her liberation from the grave, perhaps for good if we kept the devils away.

There was no house down by the beach where we could live, so I had to share the cabin with Elena to protect her against prowlers and thieves. Nothing was safe from the beachcombers at that time. There was a long concrete pier reaching into the water. On the landside, there were still a few broken cement walls standing from an abandoned factory, which I intended to use in the construction of my hangar building and laboratory for biologic research and X-ray work.

My first work was to level the ground. This done, I

rolled the plane into the ruins. Mario Matina, who had married Elena's sister Nana, helped in doing this. Now I began to build with rocks, cement, beach sand and sea water a square of walls, with a large opening on the leeside, large enough for the plane to get out of the building and onto the wide cement runway slip. I had built the plane strong enough so that I could construct my beams from the top of the walls across the middle, allowing them to rest temporarily on the plane, so as to form a working floor for erecting the roof. After the roof was supported and fastened securely on top of the cement walls I freed the ship of its additional load. I did all of this work myself, in addition to attending to Elena inside the ship, as best as I possibly could. It gave me great satisfaction to build this lab, for, was it not for her sake, all of this work? Yes, and I always had the feeling that she was helping me. She was indeed helping me with all the money I had piled up around her lovely form. She knew that this was to be her castle, her birthplace for a new life, from where she would fly away with me across this wide expanse of ocean to a better world.

There was still metabolism in her body, as the chemical reactions indicated, and this would require attention. There was always a surprise awaiting me when I opened her casket; particularly so when she had been sealed up. She certainly did not like that. I was glad when at last the house was finished and I could leave her exposed to open air. There was no more danger of deterioration except from insects which I kept away with double screens. In an airtight metal container, the gases exhaled by the body are not carried off by diffusion but accumulate and condense, into liquid form. This corrosive liquid attacks body tissues as well as the metal container, except under proper laboratory conditions where the gases are carried away by a pumping apparatus.

Having laid the concrete floors, I divided the building into two sections, one side for the hangar with workshop, the other half for a laboratory, and one room where I placed my bed, a large table, the organ, and my books. In the laboratory, I installed my million-volt transformer in the middle of the floor so it would be clear of the walls and roof beams. Against the front stonewall I placed my large X-ray machine and operating table. Along the windows on the north wall I arranged the examination bench with microscopes, scales, etc. Along the division wall I mounted shelves all the way up to the top for bottles, chemicals, glassware and other supplies, with a long bench in front for analytical work. This then was the new setup where I lived all alone with my Elena. There was only one neighbor, a harmless and a friendly man named Frank. Frank was an Italian fisherman who had built his own shack up against the wall of my building, as he wanted to be with me. Inside of the large hangar I installed my electric generating plant with switchboards right against the sea wall. This supplied all the light and power which I required; I wanted to be independent of the city electric system. The hangar could be closed up with two folding steel doors as high as the surrounding walls. The clear space above, forming a high gable, which I closed up with numerous window panels, admitted plenty of light into the entire building in addition to the windows below.

It was with great relief that at last I had my

equipment in working order and ready to use. My most important work was now to assemble all parts of the incubator which I had built in the Marine Hospital. Here, now, with my electric power plant I could finally set it in operation, something which had been delayed too long already.

All work up until now had been for the purpose of arresting and delaying further deterioration of the body tissues. Mummification had partly set in. This, however, is not beyond resurrection. The revival of the dried-up cells merely consumes more time and I never give up hope while I have a will. Now I began mixing up plasma solutions in sufficient quantities, adjusting, testing, cooling and heating elements; I also tested the circulating pumps and electron cell, sterilizing everything, including rubber and glass connectors. And last but not least, came my sweet, patiently waiting darling herself. I placed her gently into the incubator tank on a thick layer of white felt and filled the entire tank with a clear solution of oxyquinoline sulphate of sodium at a temperature of 38 centigrade, blood heat. In this solution I left her for twenty-four hours, then draining the incubator by opening the bottom valve, I refilled the tank, while the body was still wet and warm, with plasma solution of body temperature. While the tank was filling, of course, the tube of the pump intake was connected to the plasma tank until the incubator was filled up and overflowing through the foot valve into the filter and recharging tank. The outlet tube was then connected with the plasma vessel. This fluid was thus kept circulating automatically twenty-four hours a day at a temperature of 37 centigrade. Once each day I raised her body out of the incubator and permitted her to rest a little. Then I placed her on my X-ray table for a five-minute radiation with high voltage, 3 mill. Amp. 1 mm Alum, filter and then returned her immediately into the circulating plasma bath.

This process I intended to keep up as routine as long as possible, checking up on the temperature and reaction of the fluid every day, adding distilled water, glucose, saline, calcium, or whatever else was needed. Sometimes I had to neutralize the solution by adding hydrochloric acid.

As weeks passed on, I noticed to my great joy and satisfaction how her form had filled out and developed. Her living contour was again restored, and she had added weight. Her limbs were filling out and her beauty became radiant, her expression showed serenity and happiness. It impressed me so much that it kept me spellbound to gaze at her over and over again in silent rapture. It had become my supreme joy to see her daily and lift the veilings to have another look at her and to see how divinely beautiful she had developed. Often I kissed her rosy lips while she was lying in her bath, thereby getting always a liberal taste of the surrounding fluid myself, which is indeed an analysis.

With horror I remembered her appalling condition when I had first taken her from the grave. With happy confidence I could now look forward to the time when I could take her out of the bath for good. Owing to some remaining defects on her left finger and right toe, caused by the burial, I wanted to continue until her total weight, would reach one hundred pounds. She now weighed ninety pounds: that meant that a gain of sixty pounds had been achieved since the beginning of the treatment. Every evening now I sat at the organ and played to her the music she loved: Beethoven, Bach or Wagner. It was not only my own fancy, but more than that: it was a means to apply the cosmic laws of vibration through harmonic sound waves. These aside with electric waves which have positive action in a status nascendi during the formation of atomic structure. There is nothing mystical or magical about this; no, it's exact science. Needless to say, vibrations of divinely inspired harmonics differ a great deal from the vulgar kind which have destructive action.

Unfortunately I was again greatly troubled by the outside world. The W.P.A. got busy with laborers to clean up the whole terrain and then build wooden sheds and cabanas near my place. Stealing and pilfering now became all too frequent. The entire area became unsafe; complaints were of no avail. Consequently the building could never be left without a guard. Either Frank or myself had to remain there to watch the place. As the conditions kept getting worse, I found it necessary for Elena's safety to interrupt the incubation, temporarily at least. Stones had been thrown through the glass windows into the room where the incubator stood. So I lifted her out, dried her with alcohol and Eau de Cologne, emptying all of the plasma fluid into glass bottles and dismantling the incubating assembly, sterilizing and packing it away. There was no way of knowing when I would be able to resume incubation, while W.P.A. had a free hand here.

She was not embalmed now after her tissues had been resurrected by the incubation period. Although her body was sterile enough, she was not safe from insects. For

123

this reason I thought it better to extend the silken layer, protection all over her body to make sure that insects should find no exposed skin surface, and also to retard desiccation. When I had completed this, I dressed her in silken garments again, with her bridal dress and veils and the crown of gold and adorned her with all her jewels and white gloves. I kept her thus, lying in state in her large bed, with flowers about her head. It was the bed I had bought for her and in which she had died. Oh, how marvelously beautiful she now looked with the white silk lace veils covering her down to her feet. She was so precious to me that I would take no risks. To guard her day and night I slept right along side of her at night, and in the daytime hardly ever went out, except to get my mail. In that case I always locked my room securely, as well as the house, the bed was always screened with treble screens. Not even Frank had ever seen her and did not know of her presence; No visitors could ever see through those screens and discover the beautiful secret. Like Ayesha in her mountain she was hiding behind the curtains, watching everything through her veils with her farseeing eyes. I had sealed her ears loosely with sterile cotton, which would still transmit sound waves, also her nostrils with a filter, which admitted air.

Wholly absorbed as I was in this, my secret life with Elena, I hardly noticed how the months passed and the years. The outside world concerned me only when it threatened us, as it did when in 1935 the big hurricane swept over Florida.

Reports from Cuba and the United States weather bureaus predicted the storm center as coming in a straight line toward Key West from the southeast. My instruments also indicated that it was approaching this way, and heading straight for South Beach where my house stood. All of Key West had been preparing for the approaching storm, closing shutters, windows and shops. All of the cabanas had already been closed up. Therefore, Frank and I hastily boarded up every window and outer door against wind and sea pressure and sand. As the building was only one foot above the high water mark, and the hurricane would raise the water up to probably ten feet, I reinforced the entrance with strong timbers. On the inside I had large crossbeams bolted down between the cement walls of the house and also between the cement floor and the roof beams of the gable. In addition, I wheeled the plane up against the inside door beams and blocked up its wheels to put a backpressure against the doors. We, Elena, I and Frank the fisherman of the beach, were locked in for the duration of the storm. My two cars, for which there was no room inside of the building, had to be left outside and exposed to the full fury of the storm; My sailboat and Frank's skiff were high and dry up on the sand close to the building. The long row of wooden cabanas and the shed belonging to the W.P.A. were all doomed to be swept away. Only the cement walls of my building could withstand the storm. Inside, I was obliged now to pack away my books and papers, microscopes, etc. up on the shelves close to the roof for safety. Elena had to be wrapped in her silken quilt as she was. I laid the crucifix on her breast and placed her in the steel casket and closed it up so she could be lifted up into the roof loft at a moment's notice if the water should rise too high inside. The organ and all heavy machinery and electrical equipment could not be moved.

My barometer showed rapidly falling air pressure all day long and still sinking hour by hour. The northwest wind blew a howling gale and it was plain to see that the hurricane was coming on. Near nine o'clock in the evening, the noise of the rattling windows and shutters and the large steel gates became a deafening roar; we could not hear ourselves speak anymore. The full force of the storm would be here in a couple of hours. I was determined to face it conscious.

Frank was convinced that we were doomed but laid down in his bunk facing his fate like a stoic. I went into my room and sat down beside Elena's casket, and, with both of my arms clasping it, I said:

"Elena, my darling, we are alone on this shore. The hurricane may free us both from this life, but we will cling together faithfully, you and I and our God. Death will not harm us, nor separate us any more. He, who has given you to me, will not reject our souls, united as they are in His undying love."

Then, seating myself at the organ beside the coffin, I began to play, while the barometer on the wall was still sinking rapidly. I began with soft duke the sacred Good-Friday-Spell from Wagner's Parsifal. It was hardly possible to hear the sound over the roar of the hurricane, but in my soul I heard every note. Then I added Vox Celeste on the second movement. It sounded very sweet, like a chorus of angels in the high "heavens, while the satanic chorus of the gale screamed against the heavenly voices of love eternal, like in a great battle.

On and on I played. My soul was all in it; now I added more voices to give the heavenly spell more power until gradually I had full organ with increasing forte. It was then as if heaven itself lent the strength of the forte to these harmonics of eternal love. At that moment nothing existed for me but the great sound which flowed from mine and Elena's souls united with the organ. And as the organ tones diminished in the finale, dying out far away into the heavens with the faintest pianissimo, there was silence outside; the great battle of nature had come to an end.

On account of this profound silence at first I thought that I had lost my sense of hearing during this battle. I waited for a while, then I arose quickly to find out what bad happened. Looking at my barometer I noticed with joy that the air pressure was rising rapidly. Then I bent down kissing Elena's coffin, embracing it, and saying:

"Elena dear, God bless you. He saved Key West and all of us! Thank God."

I went out to Frank's room on the far end of the building, calling to him:

"Frank, it is all over now!"

As in a daze the old fisher stared at me:

"I heard you play the organ. It sounded like Holy Mass in church, so I prayed. But Doc, it's all so still now, will the storm come back again?"

"No, it will not. You can safely go to sleep now.

Good night, Frank."

At midnight the wind began gently to blow from the south, indicating that the center of vacuum was about forty to fifty miles from this beach. The hurricane had taken a sharp turn in a northerly direction out to sea; it had by-passed us. Satisfied now and feeling tired I slept peacefully all night.

The next day came the sad news of the great destruction wrought in the upper Keys of Matecumbe and Tavernier, where the hurricane finally crossed over into the Gulf after suddenly turning away from Key West. Great havoc was caused there to the veterans' camp and other settlements, destroying the highway and railroad bridges. It had taken over four, hundred lives. The hurricane had isolated Key West entirely from the mainland. After opening our barricaded doors and windows again, I found no damage outside except that a thirty-foot fishing cruiser was facing me head on. It had been hurled upon my cement slip. The gale had torn it away from its anchor in deep water and stranded it here, a total wreck. On the other side of my building my two cars were still standing, but minus a brand new tire and rim which, however, could hot have been taken by the storm. There are always some people who are hiding their misdeeds by a storm. It is being held responsible for everything even though it did not even hit Key West. One nearby cabana had been burglarized and all its goods and supplies taken during that night. It belonged to a countess, visitor from

California.

After the danger was past, I opened Elena's casket

and placed her back in her bed. Now she could absorb fresh air. The W.P.A. works on the beach were resumed, which made it impossible for me to use the incubator for my Elena...Under these circumstances the desiccation required attention every second or third day I gave her an oral infusion whenever her lips became too parched, but not more than one glassful, so that her beautiful array should not be soiled. I knew that this was hardly enough to keep the body cells alive, but I hoped that at some later day I would be able to complete her incubation and then tap her circulation for a transfusion with living- blood. I knew that she had lost some of her own blood lately. When she was in the incubator, I noticed that the circulating fluid had taken a reddish color, a result of her blood becoming mixed with the fluid in the tank. As the fluid had been clear before, I examined it under the microscope which revealed the presence of blood cells.

Christmas of 1936 was now approaching, I prepared, as always, her little Christmas tree, decorating it with silver tinsel, cotton snow and with small wax candles instead of electric bulbs. I placed the tree on a bench beside her bed with little gifts, such as picture books, chocolate, cakes, cookies, perfume„soap, face powder, etc., which she liked when alive. For me she will never die, but will live on with me, and I shall always treat and respect her as a living person.

On Christmas Eve I lit the candles on the tree, there were just thirteen of them, and placing her crucifix nearby I told her:

"Elena! It is Christmas!" Then taking my seat at the

organ I played "Silent Night" until the lights on the tree were burned down. Going to her bed and seating myself beside her, I lifted her veil and kissed her on her lips:

"Elena, darling, we are all alone in this world—you and I and our God, but we are happy and contented. Let us stay together forever."

There was a small bottle of Rhine wine on the table, another Christmas gift. I opened the bottle, filled one glass; raising it with a prayer to our God for his blessing. I drank half of it and drew the other half into my mouth. Lifting her veils again, I pressed my lips firmly against hers which were open just little. Thus slowly I forced the wine into her mouth, until I felt by the passage of air that it had entered her stomach safely. The air from my lungs entered hers and caused her bosom to rise. I released my lips and she breathed the air out again, but retained all of the wine, not a single drop spilled on her bridal array. I used this method of feeding her at different times with certain solutions when I wanted to be sure they went home where I wanted them to.

Of course, there was no risk of infection whatever, as Elena's body was now aseptic. Her nostrils were sealed with cotton but her ears were now open. While seated close to her, I noticed what seemed like a faint breathing movement of her breast, and by looking closer I found just a few drops of fresh blood running out of the corner of both eyes and both ears. I had to get some cotton to wipe it off and deposit it on a couple of microscopic slides. No further discharge was visible. I got my stethoscope to listen to her chest for a while.

There was no regular heartbeat, but there was a sound of flowing liquid in the vessels, then a pause, then a sound of flowing again with some kind of an irregular flutter in between.

Her body was still warm to the touch since the incubation, but she had already lost considerable of her blood temperature. It was only natural that she was gradually cooling out again. To slow this down as much as possible I covered her over completely with the blue silk quilt, at least for the duration of the cool weather.

During the night, I meditated for hours about this fresh red blood. What did it mean? Why should she emit blood without any blood pressure in her system? I decided to make a further investigation, and the next day I found that a scant menstrual blood discharge had taken place. Also fresh red blood had leaked from the saphenous veins on her legs, which had to be cemented with silken patches. It was all-important now to keep her safe by retaining all of the liquids in her body. With all those gangs of workers disturbing the quietude of our beach, I had to be prepared to place her back again in the hospital cabin of her airship and to take her away to a safer place.

The W.P.A. had obtained the beach from the city to improve it. Most unfortunately the person in charge of this work held a personal grudge against me, because I refused to contribute to certain cheap politicians, whose main object was to make money. These political bosses were determined to drive me from my house; in fact, they had me dynamited from my home. They, however, had no knowledge of my holy secret which I was guarding so patiently.

131

One morning my walls were shaken by the big explosions. The great concrete pier close to my house had been blown up by them. This made it impossible to live there any longer in safety. My house, now no longer protected from the sea, had to be abandoned. I received no compensation for this loss, nor provided with another house I could move into, which absolutely amounted to persecution.

At last I found another building which was large enough, where I could move in with all my possessions. There was a scarcity of houses at the time and I was glad to take it, although it was not a suitable place for my laboratory and hangar. It took me and Frank a full month to pack up and to move my twenty truckloads of equipment, from

April 30th to May 28th, 1936.

Elena, of course, was placed comfortably in the cabin of her plane. Now, with the plane hitched to my car, I taxied the airship slowly along the coast on Roosevelt Boulevard to the building on Flagler Avenue. She was the last to leave. It was a large shed, situated among bush and jungle scenery. As it consisted of only two small rooms beside the shed, I made one of them the bedroom and the other a laboratory and storeroom which, however, could only hold my X-ray equipment. The organ I placed in the bedroom, also my books, a writing table and the microscopes, etc. Frank, who had moved with me, rigged up a table, seats and shelves and some sort of a camp stove in the garage building where he could cook to his heart's delight. The three boats Frank sailed over and anchored them beside the nearby laguna among the mangroves. Here he could go out fishing as usual, catching crawfish and plenty of other kinds; but his beloved conch shells were rather scarce in this locality. Close to the house and kitchen, we planted vegetables, papayas, bananas, lime and cocoanut trees; there was plenty of wood here to keep the fire going. The kitchen door, opposite the main building, we always left open as a shelter for our dogs which guarded our home.

When everything was nice and clean inside the tiny bedroom and the doors and windows had been tightly screened, I opened the airplane to take out my secret treasure. I would not leave her a minute longer lonely by herself. Carrying her in my arms, I placed the coffin on my table and opened the six padlocks. After unfolding of the new blue silk quilt, she came out beautiful, radiant as ever with her jewels, flowers and bridal array. Here she could now breathe fresh air again, which she needed as the air inside had acid odor.

My power generating machinery could not be installed at the new place; I was unable to use it, consequently, I could incubate no more until I had built another laboratory. I decided that it was best to leave Elena exposed to the open air for a time. I knew well that it was impossible to prevent desiccation of the tissues, and that mummification would finally take place, because the small quantities of liquids I could infuse would not be sufficient to prevent it. But as long as I could prevent re-infection of the body tissues with bacteria, I was satisfied. There was nothing to prevent re-incubation later on, the most important thing now was to protect and guard her carefully against destruction.

In her big bed, covered by double and treble screens all around and a waterproof tent above it, she was secure and she looked comfortable and contented just as if she knew. And I am positive that she did know she was lying on her own mattress on which she died and was inviting me to her side. Now I slept by her side to be close to her and to protect her from insects and other dangers, as I had promised her I would do. She could not feel any injury but I could feel it for her. Whenever I discovered another leakage, I sealed it up right away with silk and wax, to stop any plasma from running away. When any part had shrunk in by the loss of fluids, I filled it up with soft sterile cotton packing and overlaid it with silk and wax. Now she could get no more radiation as I had no electricity yet, except my small windmill generator on top of the kitchen which was barely enough, when there was any wind, to keep my automobile batteries charged.

Every evening I played organ music for her and in the morning, when I had cooked my breakfast, consisting of eggs, toast and Lipton's tea, I carried it into her room and placed it on her little bedroom table. Lifting the veil I invited her:

"Come, darling, join my breakfast, our wedding breakfast."

Then, sitting down, I ate in perfect peace and contentment as I felt that she was with me and could see me. I always experienced a feeling of harmony and silent happiness as though an angel were present. Generally at noon, Frank came back from his trip with nice fresh fish and made a fish dinner with potatoes and cabbage or macaroni, so we both had our dinner in the "dog kitchen," so called by me as my dogs claimed it as theirs. These dogs, a mixture of shepherd and pointer, were very much attached to me. They consisted of Granny, the head of the dog family, and her children, a male and a female, the latter became the mother of thirteen fine, healthy pups. Granny, who was very intelligent, begged me a few times to let her come into Elena's room. When I saw how interested and anxious she seemed to be, I let her in to satisfy her curiosity. She nosed her way past the X-ray machine, then past the organ, straight to Elena's bed and sat down there, looking up at the screen expectantly and wagging her tail, then, looking at me, as if to say:

"Let me see what you have there."

I told her:

"This is your mistress, Granny, and she also likes dogs, but don't wake her up now. You may look at her through the screen, that's all." At this she raised up to a sitting position holding her paws carefully in the air so as not to touch the bed and looked through the screens. That was all she wanted. She was satisfied now and I told her:

"You watch and guard your mistress always."

All these animals proved to be good friends and always kept a faithful watch.

On the 29th day of July, 1936, I woke up early in the morning. My eyes were wide open; I was in the full possession of my senses and faculties. No matter what people will think or say: I was ready to go out and report the news to the press that Elena had at last re-awakened to life. This re-awakening was so real that I convinced myself it was not just an apparition or imagination. It was her own real body, her own personality.

As I looked at her, I noticed the fingers of her right hand moving, and on taking her hand in mine, I felt how it relaxed and became soft again. Immediately thereafter her whole arm lifted itself up and her hand pressed firmly against my face and lips as she used to do when alive, so that I should kiss it. When I kissed her hand, she opened her eyes and looked at me intently. Then, turning herself on her side toward me, she attempted to get up. I was fully awake and became alarmed, fearing that she would collapse and fall, so I spoke to her quietly:

"God bless you, Elena. I am so happy you are awakened from your long sleep."

She answered:

"I've come to you to stay for a while and keep you company."

"Elena," I answered, "it is five years that I have waited by your side for your awakening, now don't be too hasty in getting up. It may exhaust your strength, my darling. Wait a little and I will make you some hot beef tea to strengthen you."

I went out at once and made hot beef tea from Liebig's Extract. When I returned in a few minutes to give her the beef tea, I found here in a state of rigidity, but still in the same position in which I had left her and looking toward me. I turned her gently back on her cushions to straighten her and gave her the hot beef tea, tasting it first myself as usual. Then I waited by her side for some time, but she remained motionless; so it transpired that this wonderfully happy awakening had ended.

It gave me a lot to think of. This was metaphysical from every angle. Critically gathering and analyzing my own thoughts and movements during this phenomenon in order to detect any possible fault on my part at this crucial moment, which might have caused her to revert to her former state.

Was it perhaps my hesitation in the face of this unexpected phenomenon taking place? Of course, there were the physical reasons, such as the absence of blood pressure.

Or was it because I left her side that her life ebbed away?

I had heard of similar cases in my psychological studies, all of which I weighed carefully. I remembered now that, when I saw her move, my heart was beating so powerfully strong and loud for joy that I thought it would burst. This seemed natural and also in such a case, that my first duty consisted in helping her. The possibility that it all had been a dream had to be ruled out by finding her still in the same position.

I could not help feeling remorse at the thought that I may have failed somewhere to assist in the accomplishment of a miracle, and permitted it to come to naught. The mystery of the missing link in the metaphysical chain will eventually be found I am sure, obscure as it is at present. I think I can see where it can be found.

At the present time, with all of my electrical indicating and other scientific instruments dismantled, I cannot make accurate experiments, not until such a time as I have another laboratory building. For the time being, I can only confine myself to recording events as they occur by observation.

Left in charge of this end of the island of Key West by Mr. Porter, I often made inspection tours around a mile in all directions. In doing so, I discovered a wild garden of flowering myrtle bushes, growing profusely among the jungles. These evergreen bushes were loaded with strong fragrant, little white flowers. Every day when returning I brought home with me bunches of those sweet smelling flowers and placed them around Elena's head. I often placed a whole wreath of them over her hair, besides placing vases full of them on her bed table and my writing desk, and they perfumed the entire room. After a while I discovered that she had absorbed the fragrance of the flowers and exhaled it. Finally she, her bed, the organ and everything smelled like this exquisite perfume.

Work was to be done now; my boats heeded attention. I could not remain in this place forever, because I needed a laboratory again for my special research work. I intended to buy land on another island where I could build as soon as I-had sufficient capital. I needed my boats for the transportation of my goods. I thought that I would fit up the large boat with a cabin for sleeping accommodations for three persons besides cargo space, and equip it with sails as well as motor power. I also intended to equip the sailboat with a motor and add a cabin, as I intended to use it as a fishing boat in all kinds of weather. It was very strong and safe and could serve as an excellent lifeboat.

While faithfully attending to Elena, I found that more leaks had developed where plasma had run out onto the muslin gauze with which I had wrapped her body beneath her garments. It was strange that this should occur despite the precaution which I had taken of sealing her entire body with silk and wax; I made a thorough examination. It revealed that the leaks were caused by a very small insect larvae of the gnat type, a bloodsucker, which had drilled several pinholes through those protective walls in order to feed on plasma. So my good lady had to take a bath of chinosol for a few hours, so as to remove any hiding larvae. This also contracted the perforations. After being dried with alcohol and Eau de Cologne those pinholes had to be sealed up again. Then I discovered that I was all out of silk. My supply had become depleted and here Elena came to my rescue by saying to me:

"Take my bridal dress. It's soiled anyhow."

I answered: "That's a good idea, darling, I will take your bridal dress and cut out the soiled parts and there will still be plenty silk left, and I will buy a new one for you tomorrow."

Now I had more than enough silk to cover her entire body for the second time and I proceeded to do so from her neck to her feet. This layer I sealed again with wax and balsam. She was doubly secure in her two silk skins. Her body was lovely and smooth, like the skin of an infant, and she was all ready to be dressed up again. Once more I bought her a beautiful golden colored silk dress, trimmed with white silk lace; it matched the gold in her twenty-two carat golden crownlet and with fragrant white myrtle wreath around her auburn hair. Where was there ever such a lovely bride? I doubled the veils and tucked them carefully around her entire form inside her large bed, in order to double the protection of the surrounding mosquito curtain. Now I was contented and could relax and sleep well at night, knowing that she was safe. I then had a remarkable dream which I wrote in a letter to my sister; here is the copy:

Key West, June 1st, 1938.

Dear Sister:

Last night I had a dream but it seemed more like reality. I spent the whole night with father and mother. Elena, too, was with me and at my right side; Mother was at my left, and Father was facing me. We were all happy. Father appeared to be quite young. We were talking quietly and peacefully, when Elena, who had been in a death coma like, woke up suddenly. She rose up and stood before us stretching herself, smiling as happy as a child. Surprised, I warned her to be careful, as she was weak after lying down for so many years. She answered:

"Oh no, Daddy. I am calling you Daddy because you look older than your father. I am strong now. I can walk safely. Oh, I am so happy."

"All right, darling," I said, "Father will assist you and see that you don't fall."

It was wonderful to see her elation in this new world. She was wearing a new pink dress. The color of her eyes had changed from dark brown to blue. Father still had his blue-grey eyes and Mother had her brown eyes, but her hair was still dark brown. I noticed that nobody's feet touched the ground. In fact, there was no ground. We were standing in space. The most serene peace prevailed and seemed to penetrate the very atmosphere. There was a distant sound immensity, eternity, millions of harmonies from this endless space striking the very foundation of our souls; it moved our souls deep down. This really was the home of souls. This newly found home I got into was such a perfect reality, that on waking this morning, I realized how miserable this short life is down here, which luckily lasts but a brief spell. It seemed to me like an ugly dream which really it is, while there is true eternity, the infinite goal of our real happy existence forever.

It impressed me so powerfully at awakening, when returned from that brightest space of heaven into this gloomy little room called our earthly life; it almost disgusted me to be back in this life's troubles and miseries. The Indian Sanskrit calls it "Devachan," this "Home of Souls," known more than seven thousand years. When I entered it, Elena seemed to be attached to my body, which, of course, is not surprising since I had promised her that wherever I went I would take her with me. However, I failed to see Gusi and her boy, and Christa, nor any of Elena's relatives. The details of this conversation are already rapidly disappearing in the day memory, but the impression of this mighty eternity beyond will remain with me forever. Perhaps I should not speak about it, but as no

141

warning was given me, I will write it down for you before it disappears as much as the poor vocabularity of this language permit. It may interest you in case anything should happen, and also for your own sake, too.

Now, as I write this down, I have, a feeling that I have been moved and am still standing right on the threshold of this eternal space. It is as if only a thin veil separates me from it. I am convinced now that Mother and Father are living happily together in that eternal life, and I am so glad that it has moved so close to me or else I have moved close to it.

With love,

Your brother Carl.

The only thing on that morning's awakening which consoled me was Elena. On seeing her back again at my side, I said:

"All right, my darling, we will carry on the fight together until we go back. The time is short, then we shall be together in the home where there is no death."

Seeing her crucifix on the side of the bed and Saint Cecilia above, playing the organ, I sat down at the organ by the bed and played the hymn "The Home of the Soul." It sounded well enough, but oh, how poor compared to what I had heard in the immensity of sounds of the infinite. The nearest resemblance to it would be an immense radio where you would hear millions of voices together from all parts of the world in peaceful harmony. There must be a possibility to tune an organ to a kind of sound which have deep metaphysical action on the soul. Seemingly impossible, I still would try it if I had time to do it. For this reason, I had tuned Elena's organ particularly careful with a kind of a tone according to my own hearing, that it sounded in accord with mine and Elena's inner soul. Such an instrument practically needs constant care to keep it in a fit condition, and requires a lot of patience; it is useless to try tuning when not at perfect peace or in too much of a hurry. When playing, this organ in the evening I could distinctly hear Elena's voice singing, accompanying the organ tone whenever I played one particular song, namely:

"Ach wie ist's moglich dann, dass ich Dich lassen kann," "How can I part from Thee, how can I leave Thee?"

It sounded so sweet and lovely when her voice joined the organ tone. In Australia I had not less than three different organs which I all kept in tune in my residence.

There was immutable friendship, love and harmony between Elena and myself. Frank, on the other hand, always seemed to have some trouble with the dogs in the kitchen, or himself, or with the townspeople. It was just his nature and he would feel ill at ease if he could not dig up a scrap, if only with the cat.

Placing Elena on the scales, I found that by degrees she was losing weight as time went on. It was desiccation. She was drying out and had been losing gradually from ninety to seventy pounds, then to sixty, then fifty and finally down to forty pounds as I weighed her from time to time. With this loss of weight her features would naturally change, becoming stiff and a little distorted when the underlying tissues fell in after dissipation of the fluids, leaving empty spaces as the water evaporated.

On the 2nd of March, 1940, while working on my large boat, stepping on deck frames from which I had removed the planks, I slipped and fell below in between the exposed floor beams, breaking my ribs on the left side near the heart. I thought my end had come as my lungs could not function, and I could not get any air. I was paralyzed with pain and unable to extricate myself.

My first thought was: My God, what shall become of Elena in the house if I do not return. My sweet Elena, I will join you soon.

Then I heard her voice say to me:

"Take a deep breath, as deep as you can, expand your chest, then you can come home."

My sweet angel had come to help and console me in my distress. As my lungs refused to expand any more and my heart was beating with difficulty, I relaxed for a few minutes to concentrate on thinking: Elena, you are right, it will work or else it will burst.

I tried to take a breath, but couldn't as my chest was collapsed and my heart was pounding with excruciating pain. Freeing myself a little with my arms, which were also injured, from the timbers, I lay still for another minute, then I started again with all the strength that I could summon to expand my chest. I managed to get a little air into my lungs and found that it helped me. I tried again to get more air, and with all available force succeeded in fully inflating my lungs so that my chest now became fully expanded. I felt that the broken ribs had aligned themselves normally again without cutting internally; this because the pain had now become less intense. It was just bearable and I was able to climb out of the boat and walk home, always keeping my chest filled with air to prevent it from collapsing again. When I got to the house, I had to lie down alongside of Elena to rest. I said:

"Elena, my angel, I am back by your side. I don't care what happens next since I am with you."

The pain was becoming almost unbearable as the blood began circulating. Finally I had to get up again. I did not have sufficiently wide adhesive tape for bandage and had to wait until a tourist brought some from town. Then I bandaged my chest myself, but still the pain kept agonizing me in every position, either sitting or lying down, flat on my back or on rolling to my left or right side; it made not a bit of difference. That night I heard Elena's voice again:

"Come closer to my side, then turn so that your back lies against my body."

I answered:

"Darling, I certainly will do anything to get rid of this pain."

Slowly moved over until my back was resting snugly against the right side of her body. All pain left me immediately. Oh, how thankful I was to have found relief. I thanked God and my Elena. At last I could go to sleep in peace and breathe normally without any pain. I slept well, forgetting the injury until late the next day. Only, when I moved away from her, the pain returned. So, when evening came, I had to lean against her again to be free from pain. It was strange that as soon as my back touched her body, the pain promptly left. This continued every night until my chest was completely healed. During all this time, I could not lie in any other position.

As I was still too weak to work on the boats, I passed my time in making new cement urns and vases to beautify Elena's tomb, which would also be mine some day. I also remolded the figure of the angel above the entrance of the tomb who is holding a sealed letter. The boys had shot the wings off the angel. While thus occupied with cement work, visitors also wanted similar work for their gardens, which I did for them.

On three, successive days, namely September 11th, 12th and 13th, 1940, while lying half awake, I heard Elena's voice anxiously calling me:

"Hide me, hide me somewhere." And another time: "Can't you hide me somewhere?"

Astonished at what it might mean, because, of course, I took it literally, I answered:

"Why should I hide you, Elena? You could not be safer anywhere than here in your, own bed." It puzzled me also that she would not say anything more. Of course, I could have put her back into the casket, which would not have been better but worse; it would deprive her of the air which she needed.

The 14th of September, just before sunrise, I was awakened by Elena's body trembling all over for about a minute. I tried to soothe her trembling form with my hands and spoke to her softly:

"Elena, God bless you, darling, are you going to rise?

146

Rise, if it must be to our Heavenly Father. All of my love will help you on the way. When I took her hands in mine and kissed her lips, the tremor had gone.

CHAPTER IX

THE BREAKING OF THE PEACE

On the 28th of September, the tomb in the cemetery had been broken into and the coffins been tampered with. I learned of this from Nana's husband. Arriving at the tomb,

I found Elena's sister Nana there with some other women, the sexton and undertaker Pritchard. Both of the latter assured me that everything was all right inside, as the inner coffin had not been opened and that they had closed the outside casket. And that henceforth the tomb would be watched. Whereupon Elena's sister Nana insisted that the vault be opened as she wanted to see inside the coffin. With this I flatly refused to comply.

On the 1st of October, 1940, I was again called to the cemetery by Nana's husband and there was Nana, urging me to open the coffins in the vault. This time there was more of a crowd. I had the only keys to my vault. Nana threatened that if I did not open the coffins for her, she would have them opened by order of, the law. Suspecting her immediately of breaking into the vault in the first place, I absolutely refused to open the tomb any more, as there were no reasons to disturb the coffins. Nana then said, spitefully, that if she had her way, she would take Elena out of the tomb and bury her in a hole in the earth to rot like herself, and whatever Elena had said to me were lies. She did not want Elena to lie in this elaborate tomb, that she was no better than herself, why should she lie in state.

"Let her rot in the earth like myself." I answered:

"You ought to be ashamed of yourself, talking like that at the grave of Elena. She is an angel, but not you. I can clearly see that you don't love her, nor are you interested in her safety. All you seem to be interested in is to strip your sister again of her jewels, that's why you broke into the tomb."

The sexton had handed me a piece of rusty iron, bent from the strain of wrenching the locks from the cement walls, and a pair of old rusty scissors, used apparently to dig the window panes out of the door. These I turned over to the sheriff for fingerprints. (No fingerprints were taken, however).

After a while Nana spoke again, but this time plaintively:

"Please, open the tomb and let me see Elena inside the coffin or I believe I will go crazy. If only I could see her to know that she is all right, I'll be satisfied."

Well, this sounded sensible, and fearing that she really might become hysterical and since she was the only sister remaining, I decided to convince her and let her see that Elena was perfectly safe. So I said to her:

"All right. Nana, I don't want you to go crazy, I will let you see Elena. Let us talk this over in peace and arrange it between ourselves. This is not a public affair."

"Where do you want us to go?" she asked.

"Well, to your house, which is nearest from here," I answered.

"No," she replied. "Not in my place."

"Well then, let's drive down to my house."

She agreed and so we drove straight for my house on

Flagler Avenue.

At my home she invited another woman, who was in the car, to come in which, however, I vetoed, as she did not belong to the family.

When coming inside my rooms, Nana stayed back near the door, while her young husband Mario came along with me to where Elena's bed stood. He exclaimed:

"Here is Elena's bed. Nana."

I then invited Nana:

"Come here, Nana, and see how beautiful Elena is resting in her bed in her silken garments with all her jewelry. Come and see, she could not have it better anywhere. I think that will pacify you now."

She came alongside and looked at Elena, after I had lifted the curtains. After looking her over, she turned around:

"This isn't my sister. That's another girl you have here."

Her husband, looking at her more closely now and feeling her hand and hair, said:

"Yes, Nana, it is she."

Nana turning to me, said: "How long have you got her here?"

"It is now seven years," I said.

Nana gripped her husband's arm and said:

"Let's get out of here, I feel bad. Let's go back to the cemetery and open the vault to see what is inside the coffins."

Her husband Mario answered excitedly:

"What's the use now, you have seen that she is here." But she persisted in pretending that it was not Elena and Mario shrugged:

"I don't know what to do with Nana, she's crazy."

"I think so too, but you ought to teach her some common sense," I said. "I am not going to open the vault and coffins. Not after showing Elena to her."

They both went to the car, but before going away, Nana called me:

"I want you to put Elena back into the vault, but I want to be present to see that she lies in the coffin, do you hear?"

"Elena and I will go back into the vault together when our time is up, but not right now. I don't see why you should worry about her now. You never looked after her for the past nine years. She has been under my care all these years. I have paid all of her expenses, not you; you forget that I own that, tomb with everything that is inside, not you!"

After this they drove back to town. It was the last conversation between her sister and me, and it is the absolute truth, no matter what Nana said later on at the trial.

I went back to Elena and said some soothing words to her, lest she be hurt that her sister would not acknowledge her.

"She cannot injure us, no matter what comes, don't worry, darling. And as Nana is only after your jewels, let me take care of them for you until the trouble is past, then you will get them all back, sweetheart."

She released them easily and I locked them safely away in a little casket.

On Sunday, the 5th of October, 1940, there drove up the fateful motorcade, headed by two sheriffs, then the justice of the peace, followed by the funeral car and several other cars, all halting at my place. The two sheriffs, stepping forward, knocked at my entrance door. When I opened the screen, the head sheriff presented a warrant on which I was charged with being in possession of a dead body. Politely he asked whether I was the person whose name was on this paper. I answered yes, this was my name. He then asked me to show him the body. After seeing the body in the bed, he inquired if it was true that I had this body in my possession for seven years. I answered in the affirmative.

"And who is she?"

"She is my bride, Elena Hoyos."

He asked further whether I had a certificate for the body.

"Yes, I have."

"Show it to me, please."

After getting out her certificate from Elena's records, I showed it to him. He shook his head:

"This is her certificate of death, that isn't the certificate we want."

"I do not know of any other certificate required for the dead."

"I am sorry, we have to take you to the courthouse, as, you have no certificate. You may explain in court."

So I followed the sheriff into their car. I noticed the funeral car driving up and two attendants stepping in my door. They carried Elena out in a wicker basket, putting her in the funeral car. This audacity enraged me. I made a move to stop them. The sheriffs held me on each side, pacifying me, telling me everything was all right, but I said:

"There is no security for my house, when strangers are going in and out at liberty. I protest against this violation of my rights."

The sheriff answered: "We are having the body placed in the funeral home where it is safer until your case is settled. Then, you may get it back. I will see that nothing is removed and lock the doors and bring you the keys."

After bringing me the keys, the car started toward town, where I was taken to the courthouse.

Now there began cross-examination by the sheriff. All about my past experience with Elena, her death, burial and disinterment, reinterment in the tomb, etc., etc. Finally he dug out the great old U.S. Law Statute book, showing me the paragraph under which I had been indicted, according to the warrant, reading it to me:

"Accused of wantonly and maliciously demolishing,

disfiguring and destroying a grave."

The sheriff was a kind-hearted man; I saw how his eyes filled with tears as he said:

"I see there is a wrong being done to you, you are not guilty in the sense of the charges in the book. You did build the tomb and made it beautiful at your own expense. I am sorry, but we have to keep you here until the case is cleared in court."

By this time the place was crowded with photographers, taking shots from right and left. It annoyed me and I asked the sheriff, why all this publicity. He answered smiling:

"They are photographers of the press."

"Why do you permit this nuisance?"

"Well, it is a custom, our liberal government gives freedom to the press."

Then came the order by Justice of Peace, Esquinaldo, that I be held on $1000 bail until the court's disposal of the case.

I was taken into the county jail for retention. But first I handed the sheriff Elena's jewel case to lock up in the office safe. I had picked it up at home before leaving and I didn't like taking it with me to the jail. I also asked the sheriff to take care of my dogs, which he promised.

This night in jail was hard for me. When I laid down on the cot, staring at that barred window, I finally prayed:

"If this is to be my final end, then, God, unite me with my Elena forever, as a spiteful world makes our peaceful existence impossible."

A band began playing somewhere in the neighborhood. It was a cradle song, over and over again, to lull me to sleep. Suddenly Elena's spirit was standing before me in her bridal dress, bending down, embracing and kissing me:

"Suffer it for me, it won't be long, then you will be free." Then it was dark again. As she had become invisible, I turned over with my face against the wall, as I did not want to see the bars. I slept peacefully until morning.

As soon as I woke up, a friend came. Looking through the iron-barred window, he comforted me, offering help. Shortly after breakfast more friends arrived, offering help, asking me if they could bring some fruits and milk, and informing me that Frank would stay on my premises on guard day and night until my return. They promised to bring food for him as well as for the 13 dogs. Now this was quite a substantial help to me. I had not known I had such good friends. In the afternoon a lady was brought in by the jail keeper, who handed me fruit and sweets and also promised to see that my place and the dogs were taken care of. And in the evening I was surprised by the Good Samaritan, Senorita Marguerita, and a young Spanish friend, who knew Elena well. She consoled me kindly, bringing cookies, fruit, sweets and hot tea for my supper. With my Elena taken from me, I had felt utterly lost; now I learned there were good people left in this world.

This night the mysterious band again played the same cradle song somewhere nearby and I had a good, restful sleep and a feeling that I was not forsaken. In the morning again I noticed a friendly face, looking in my barred window. After breakfast the chief sheriff came to introduce Attorney L. Harris to me. He offered to defend me in court if I would give him the authority, which I gladly did.

At noon, the keeper informed me that a whole crowd of young ladies had come all the way from Tampa, who fought demanding to see me. But he said he could not let them come inside as there were too many and they would storm the whole place. So I should better go out in the yard to meet them.

"But don't forget," he said, "they are all my girls."

I went outside to the young ladies, all pretty girls, who shouted:

"We have all come from Tampa to see you. We are cigar makers from the Tampa factory, and we have read all about you in the papers. We wish you luck and that you will win out and get your Elena back."

"We are all for you," said one pretty speaker in a beautiful black silk dress.

They were such a delightfully happy lot, and they all shook hands with me while I expressed my delight in their coming and thanked them for their kind wishes. Meanwhile these good girls were making a collection among themselves, offering it to me, which I refused to accept but was obliged to take, as they insisted. The kind offer proceeded from generous hearts and it would have offended them if I had not accepted, so there was no use arguing.

They finally took leave with kind and sincere wishes. How nice and sweet it was of these young girls, who were motivated by true benevolence. God will be with them all and bless them.

In the afternoon came Father Moreaux, the priest who baptized Elena. He offered his help, but I did not see any need for help for myself.

"I am all right. The one who needs help and protection and who cannot defend herself is Elena, since she has been taken away from me."

He said he thought she was safe enough while in the custody of the undertaker where she was now, but I had my doubts. And later it proved that I was right. Therefore, I wrote a letter and sent it out by the warden to the Sister Superior of the convent, who knew Elena well before death, imploring the Sisters to protect Elena while she was away from my care.

A lady came from Miami to interview me, bringing chocolates and fruit for my supper, telling me she would stay for the court hearing, before going back. In the evening Marguerita came again, untiring angel, bringing nice hot tea and biscuits, my favorite food, and also presenting me with a rosary. Senorita Marguerita knows me well from the hospital.

Again the band played the same tune that night.

On the 8th of October, Attorney Harris, led me into the courthouse to a seat near the platform. It was to be a preliminary hearing before the Justice of Peace, Esquinaldo.

The hall was packed with people. After the formal reading of charges against me by the State Attorney, he called Mrs. Medina, Elena's sister, as chief witness. She told how I alone had the key to the mausoleum and always kept it locked up, and that I always, refused to open it when she wanted to go in. (The fact is, that frequently I opened the tomb, so that the relatives could go inside, but never once did they do so.)

She added that people had been talking in town and she wanted to see if Elena was safe. But that, instead, I had suggested to talk things over. So she and her husband went with me to my house on Flagler Avenue. There she said she caught a glimpse of the old wooden bed her father gave her when she was sick. (It was I who bought this bed for Elena.) Raising the curtains, she said, she saw the feet of the body.

"That's Elena," she quoted me as saying. "I beg you to leave her to me, see how pretty she looks, touch her little hands." She claimed to have answered: "You have caused us lots of trouble, people are talking about us. They say, you have a ring and talk to her by wireless." And I had answered, "You don't have to listen to people." Also she declared, she had given me an ultimatum, namely, that I must place Elena back in the tomb within a week or else she would proceed against me. And at the end of the week she got the warrant, which brought my arrest the following Sunday. Miss Medina, a friend of hers, corroborated her

159

story, as did her husband Mario Medina.

Then Mrs. Sawyer, custodian of the Catholic part of the cemetery, testified to finding the glass door on the vault broken and she had informed Mrs. Medina, which in turn prompted her to question me.

Asked by the judge if she knew who broke into the vault, she answered:

"I don't know."

Otto Bethel, sexton of the cemetery, verified the date of the burglary in the cemetery. Reginal Pritchard of the funeral home, employed by me to conduct Elena's funeral and later disinterment for transfer into the mausoleum, was the only defense witness. Pritchard testified that Elena's father had signed the authorization before he died, for a disinterment to be conducted under von Cosel's supervision at his expense.

Asked by the judge how much he thought I had expended on behalf of Elena, he said:

"Close to $3000."

Asked how the remains looked to him now, he answered:

"If I went to see a wax figure at Kress or any other store, I would see the same thing."

Elena's body, laid out in a funeral parlor, dressed in her blue silk robe, with a rose in her hair, and covered by a gauze veil, was the biggest sightseeing attraction that Key West had ever known. No less than 6,850 people viewed the body. Her little patent leather shoes reposed beside her stockinged feet.

Now I had to take the chair. I gave my name, Carl Tanzler von Cosel, age 64, occupation, chemist, engineer, physicist, scientist, roentgenologist with degrees in philosophy, psychology, medicine, etc. Questioned: how I got acquainted with Elena, when and where I met her, and what Elena was to me. I answered that she was my patient and later became my bride and that I always regarded her as my wife since she accepted my ring.

"I had been in love with her the first time I saw her. I knew then she was the lady I had been looking for all my life."

I told how I had envisioned her from my early youth, painting pictures of her before I had seen her. How she appeared to me in a vision in the old Cosel manor, also in Italy in Campo Santo. How amongst the monuments and tombs, I saw her form and features carved in marble, standing on the grave of a young woman. How, while still gazing, her living spirit appeared just behind the monument and then it disappeared again.

"It was in Australia many years later when her spirit appeared in my residence in Sydney, right beside the pipe organ, her dark hair hanging over her shoulders down to her knees. The spirit stayed in my house seven days, walking with me every step."

Then Attorney Harris interrupted:

"And then you came to Key West and found that lady, the spirit of your dreams, and lost her again, didn't you?"

"Yes, sir," I said. "But she is still with me now right here in this hall. I told her, no matter what happened to her I would take care of her in life and death. This holy promise took complete control of my mind and body. She was my bride when she accepted my proposal of marriage and I regard her as my wife. Her death has sealed our bond.

"I built her monument with my own hands and watched over her all these years so that nothing should harm her, and I think that I have done my best."

"What did you find when you disinterred her? What did she look like? "

"There were plenty of maggots. Her body was teeming with them. Everything was a mess."

"How long ago was it that you took the bones out of the crypt to your house?"

"It was months after they were placed in the tomb, pretty close to eight years ago."

"How did you remove Elena's bones from the crypt to your house?"

"I removed the casket from the crypt, into a car outside of the cemetery and drove alongside the airplane, placing it in the cabin."

"Did you meet anybody during this work, did anybody help you and if so, who was the person, as the casket must have been heavy?"

"No, sir, I did not meet a living person during my

work, except the driver of the car outside, who helped me to lift the casket up into the plane, that was all, and I don't know his name."

"Didn't the taxi driver ask you what it contained?"

"No. He asked no questions, I paid for the service."

"Did you not move the airplane to the beach afterward?"

"Yes, I did. Mario Medina did the moving!"

"Medina, is that true, did you do the moving?"

"Yes, sir, I moved the airplane to the beach, but I didn't know that Elena was inside."

Harris questioned me:

"Did you have the idea that her spirit would unite with her body and commune with you?"

"Yes, so it did. Many times her spirit gave me advice, even about the organ, also technical advice. Whenever I do not know what to do, she tells me. She also told that this trouble was coming and asked me several times to hide her body, but I asked, why should I hide her, but she said no more and a week later the trouble came."

"How would it affect you if that body were taken from you?"

"I would feel lost. I had promised her I would keep and protect her against destruction for the rest of my life, even at the sacrifice of my own life. It may endanger my own life."

"How long do you think her body will last in the

condition it is now?"

"Indefinitely."

"Do you think there is still life in the body which could be resurrected?"

"There is always life left in the body which can be resurrected by special methods, such as incubation, but as I had been interrupted repeatedly I could not complete my work, though partly successful. I can do better yet, if I am left undisturbed in my research."

On the 9th of October, after the hearing; I was informed of the Court's decision: that I be held further under $1,000 bail until the next session of the criminal court, one month later, on the charge of wantonly and maliciously destroying a grave and removing the body without authorization. This was read to me by Judge Lord from the law books. Also I was informed that I would see Elena no more, as she was no relative of mine. I was just a friend and that was all, and she was not going to be put back into the vault, but would be buried in the ground by the sister, Mrs. Medina.

I was thunderstruck. This was not fair, this was monstrous. She to be buried again after all my work? Elena nothing to me? She, who was everything to me? All I could stammer was:

"It is the end of everything for me. I protest against this inhuman decision. You cannot do this. It means her utter ruin and a break of faith to my Elena. If I cannot have her back, I will abide by your decision, but I will carry on my fight to the highest court of the land to annul this decision."

Later, Attorney Harris came into my cell with some moving picture agent, who wanted to produce a film of the affair. Harris advising me to accept on a percentage basis, because it would bring in money and he would place the bond to free me. But after I had given my consent to the undertaking, the man told Harris, that, as far as he was concerned, I might as well stay in prison, until he wanted me.

The 10th of October, Thursday, I was called to the courthouse to be examined by three doctors, for sanity, by order of the court. They declared me perfectly sane, there could be no other finding, despite a few cranks who would like to see me declared insane.

The doctors later examined Elena's body at the undertaker for signs of violation which was the judge's order. This examination, too, proved negative as they reported, the body being mummified.

Visitors continued to call on me in the jail. They brought fruit and chocolate, and the sweet Senorita Marguerita brought hot tea and biscuits for my supper in the evening again.

And the invisible band still played that cradle song each night until I fell asleep.

At last, on Saturday, October 12th, I was called by the sheriff to the office. Friends had placed the bond for me, (but not the moving picture agent). They were Benny

Fernandez and Joseph Zorsky, who had made the following statement:

"Persons in Key West who recall the circumstances surrounding Dr. von Cosel's kindly administrations while Elena Hoyos was in the hospital, have implicit faith in his motives. In appreciation of the services he rendered then, for the devotion to the girl he loved, and because of the humanitarian aspects of this present case, I have followed my best judgment in assisting in furnishing bond for the defendant. We, who know him, think he should be freed of all charges."

Attorney Harris received many heartening letters from citizens all over the country, such as:

Will you please bring this letter to the attention of the proper authorities. Relative to Carl Tanzler von Cosel, we feel that the very fact that he preserved and kept a human body for a period of seven years is proof of his abilities as a scientist; furthermore, his investigation into the supernatural should be considered as humane and valuable and not as a criminal case. We resent any calumny as to his mental status and we protest against the arrest and imprisonment of a man of noble character and intent. In these times; when the world's lust goes out to kill and to destroy, it is no more than to be expected that an innocent man suffers persecution. But, if by a miracle a person like Prof. von Cosel would succeed in restoring to life a deceased person, the greatest discovery of all ages would have been made.

Even if his chances be a million to one against success, it is worthwhile to try. Let not the 20th century prosecute a scientist in his research. Past history reveals that most of our great scientists have been unjustly treated by the majority, who could neither follow nor comprehend men, who had the courage and intelligence to further the progress of the world.

Summing up, we feel that Professor Carl von Cosel, since the laws of these States made it impossible for him to receive permission to carry on his line of research, has had no recourse except to do exactly what he has done.

We feel that not only should he be liberated with compensation, but also, that he should be permitted to carry on with his studies with the permission of the subject's custodians.

Signed: L. and L. and S.

Of New York and Florida.

I was free now. All I wanted was to go home. But my friends, Zorsky and Benny, would not let me go. Their car was waiting outside to take me to their hotel, the Cactus Terrace, where I was invited to stay as their guest and recuperate a while, for I needed rest. They all tried to cheer me up and they protected me from curiosity. Many tried to see me by all kinds of maneuvers, but in vain. I had had enough cross-examination and was tired of it. I sorely needed rest though I never refused friendly conversation with honest people or with scientists.

But all the time I was pining to be back in the room again, where Elena's bed stood, despite the excellent comforts here in the hotel and the kind hospitality. There was a mysterious force; it was Elena herself, which urged me to come back to where she had been with me. So, on October 19th, I went home to take charge of my premises and give Frank, who had been guarding the place day and night, a well-deserved rest. There I found, in the meantime, that almost half of my dogs had died, amongst them "Granny," my good, old faithful Granny.

Out of the blue, the movie man reappeared. He wanted to rig up some kind of an outdoor stage, in the woods, close to the building, for the purpose of producing a moving picture of his own, with me in it as an actor (which I am not). However, it proved a failure from the start. I did not approve of the whole silly performance. Besides the contract had never been fulfilled; in my hour of need this man had failed to put up the thousand-dollar bond for me as he had promised to do.

By hundreds and thousands people came to see me at my hermitage in Flagler Avenue. The license plates of their cars represented every state in the Union and there were visitors from the Bahamas, from Cuba and from Canada. They were nice, kindhearted people all of them and full of sympathy. It made me feel glad after this unpleasant experience. Folks came to shake hands with me and to see the airplane and the organ, to take pictures and even movies in Technicolor. I took this as an homage for my darling Elena and it made me proud. Some asked for flowers, others took along some small discarded organ parts. Ladies begged for tiny bits of Elena's bridal dress for a souvenir; even nails and screws of my laboratory were in demand. I hadn't thought I would like visitors, but as it turned out they did me a lot of good.

Soon I was able to provide appropriate little gifts; pictures of Elena and some of the plaster of Paris death masks I had made from her.

For months on end this public interest set new records for traffic on the highways and on the toll-bridges leading to Key West. People began to tell me that I had "put Key West on the map." But although it was a pleasure and a comfort to me to find that I had so many friends, there was considerable physical strain involved in this. For they came as early as dawn and they kept on coming till late at night. I hardly had any time to get a meal and they all wanted for me to tell the story; an impossible feat for me since the complete story takes hours to tell. But then; I always did the best I could and it was because so many friendly people urged me to write a book so they could read and keep the story, that I promised them that I would do so when I would have time, but at present I was much too busy.

My knees had to serve me as a desk to write the book of Elena. Her body is gone, but then the casket is still by my side and in it I have placed her plaster form of her body clothed in the last of her three bridal gowns. The lid is lined with her pictures when alive and at all times there are fresh flowers by her head and the silver crucifix stands guard and Elena's rosary is draped over the shoulders of our Savior.

Human malice had dynamited my laboratory, on the beach long before; human meanness has plundered and torn down the very roof over my head. Human jealousy and hatreds have robbed me of the body of my Elena; they have even poisoned my faithful dogs.

Yet Divine happiness is flowing through me. For she is with me. Nobody could take her away from me for God

Almighty has united our souls. She has survived death, forever and ever she is with me.

And every look at her picture and every thought in my mind is a silent prayer of thanks. Thanks to the Creator who let me to find her. Thanks that He gave me the strength and the knowledge to prolong her brief life on earth for nearly two years, to make it tolerable in its pains and to salvage her beauty from the ravages of the grave.

She is my everlasting joy, she is to me that supreme and divine joy which the great Beethoven tried to express— and couldn't enjoy and feel in the last before his death, his Ninth Symphony. God bless her. *Ex tenebris lucem.*

EPILOGUE

Von Cosel ends his diary on a hopeful note: *Ex tenebris lucem* (from darkness, light) But events that unfolded in the years after he wrote his diary point more towards the darkness.

Von Cosel left Key West in 1944 and moved near Zephyrhills, Florida, living out the rest of his days near his first wife Doris and sharing his tale with visitors. Only a few people know what became of Elena, but the prevailing theory is that she was buried in a secret location; most say in the Key West Cemetery. Nana, too, succumbed to tuberculosis. Her husband was electrocuted on a construction site.

Shortly after von Cosel left town there was a mysterious explosion at Elena's grave. Perhaps her spirit breaking free, but more likely, von Cosel's way of showing Key West the true meaning of the crime for which he was tried.

In 1972, one of the doctors who examined Elena's body revealed that that count had inserted a paper tube in her vaginal area that allowed intercourse, indicating he had consummated his post mortem marriage.

Carl Tanzler von Cosel was found dead on July 3, 1952. Beside him was a life-size replica of Elena Hoyos.

Recommended Reading

Discover more details and go behind the scenes with Key West's leading authority on everything von Cosel.

WWW.BENHARRISONKEYWEST.COM

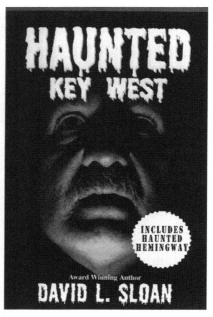

WWW.DAVIDLSLOAN.COM

Made in the USA
Columbia, SC
28 May 2021